PEP G

The Philosophy t

PEP GUARDIOLA

THE PHILOSOPHY
THAT CHANGED THE GAME

Miguel Angel Violán

Meyer & Meyer Sport

Originaltitel: El métode Guardiola

© Miguel Angel Violán, 2010

Columnia Edicions Llibres i Comunicació, S.A.U.

Peu de la Creu, 4, 08001 Barcelona

Translation: Caleb J. Moore

British Library Cataloguing in Publication Data

A catalogue record for this book is available from the British Library

Miguel Violán: Pep Guardiola – The Philosophy that Changed the Game

Maidenhead: Meyer & Meyer Sport (UK) Ltd., 2014

ISBN 978-1-78255-029-7

© 2014 by Meyer & Meyer Sport (UK) Ltd.

Aachen, Auckland, Beirut, Budapest, Cairo, Cape Town, Dubai, Indianapolis,

Kindberg, Sydney, Olten, Singapore, Tehran, Toronto

Member of the World Sports Publishers' Association (WSPA)

www.w-s-p-a.org

Printed and bound in Germany by:

B.O.S.S Druck und Medien GmbH

ISBN 978-1-78255-029-7

E-Mail: info@m-m-sports.com

www.m-m-sports.com

CONTENTS ▪ ■ ■

" I give you fans my word that we will

push ourselves. I don't know if it will

end in success, but I won't let up.

Buckle up! We're going to have fun!"

Guardiola to fans at the

2008-2009 Barça team presentation

on 16 August 2008

DEDICATION ▪▪▪

I dedicate this book to my parents, Enric Violán i Tohà (†) and María Dolores Galán Puigdevall. I also dedicate it to all of the members of my family who came before us as well as those here with us today and those who will come after us. I also dedicate this book to my wife Maria Antònia, my daughters Ariadna and Patrícia Violán i Camprubí, my siblings Enric and Núria, and my nephews Èric and Edu. I dedicate it to my parents-in-law, Esteve Camprubí and Maria Antònia Claramunt, who generously gave up their seats in the stands at Camp Nou allowing us to enjoy the game together with the 'Gómez clan'—Bernat Gómez, Montse Camprubí, Núria, Ferran and Guim.

Naturally, I also dedicate this book to my few but good friends as they are always there when I need them. Four of them have kindly agreed to contribute to this book.

Lastly, I would like to express my gratitude in general to all those who placed their trust in me and lent me their support in writing this book by providing information and sharing their views.

I admire all those who show how the world should be by the way they live their lives.

INTRODUCTION ■ ■ ■

This book is based on journalistic content gathered from print, radio, television and online sources, current sporting events (including press conferences), secondary literature as well as conversations with people associated with Pep Guardiola. The book does not contain exclusive quotations by the former Barça coach but does provide interesting information from those who are close to him. The fact that he does not grant any interviews is part of this coach's communications policy.

A major portion of this book was written at my home in Barcelona's Eixample district. I also worked in the reading rooms of the Ateneu Barcelonès, the computer room of Widener Library (Harvard University's main library), the Cafeteria of Harvard University's unique Cooperative Society located on Harvard Square, and in the greater Boston area, a crucible of knowledge in the United States.

Every line in this book bears a small reflection of these different settings although there was always a common denominator: my internet connection. That is simply a sign of the times.

THE BOY WHO CRIED FOR PINOCCHIO ■ ■ ■

(FOREWORD TO THE ENGLISH EDITION)

by Miguel Angel Violán

Picture the following scene: the Guardiola family dining room in the village of Santpedor about an hour outside of Barcelona. It's afternoon, and school is out for the day. The young Pep is sitting in front of the television. He is watching his favourite programme: The Adventures of Pinocchio. He is crying inconsolably. His mother, Dolores, comes in and asks him,

'Pep, why are you crying?'

The boy replies,

'I can't help it, Mum. So many terrible things are happening to Pinocchio…'

The tears and sensitivity are part of the essence of Josep Guardiola i Sala. They are in his DNA. They are the tears he shed as a sensitive boy when faced with the injustices of the world. It was no different with the tears that he had to hold back when he left his parents' home at age 13 for football boarding school (a school for life as well). This school would rule his life from that point onward. It was FC Barcelona's La Masía youth football academy, the wondrous blue-red talent incubator.

It is there that our protagonist's character developed. He is a man compelled by circumstance to grow up before his time.

Nonetheless, he held his great sensitivity inside through unflinching will power and the desire to keep pace with the 'tough lads' in his environment as he did what he loved most: kick the ball, play football, anytime and anywhere.

There were also those who were against his acceptance to La Masía.

'He is too frail,' they said.

'He has to stay. He has a head for the game,' reasoned youth academy manager Oriol Tort and, in doing so, made a decision that would be extremely important for Pep's future career.

Tort's decision was not based on Guardiola's extraordinary skill at heading the ball but rather on his intelligence, quick thinking, anticipation when playing and talent for delivering swift and precise passes.

Sensitivity and intelligence are what characterise the essence of Pep Guardiola's personality. All that was needed was to add his passion for football. Pep does what he loves, and he loves what he does. He has proven this sufficiently in his highly successful career up to this point, first as a player and then as coach of FC Barcelona. As the latter, he led the senior squad to take home 14 of 19 possible titles, a feat that would be very difficult to reproduce.

There have been triumphs that brought tears, now of joy, such as the victory in the World Club Championship final on 19 December 2009 in Abu Dhabi when he won his sixth title in a row within a single season.

It was an unmatched triumph and a record accomplished by no other rookie coach ever. He had just entered the stage. It was extraordinary, an unprecedented success, and absolutely meteoric. It was by rights something reserved for those chosen for glory. Guardiola's life is a symbol of unadulterated passion for the game of football. It is a passion of superlative proportions that at times seems almost obsessive. In any case, it made its presence felt very early in Guardiola's life. Pep's mother recalls how he kicked incessantly in the womb. He was a footballer before he was born!

The walls of the Plaça dels Ases de Santpedor (Guardiola's birthplace) could bear witness to the thousands of times that Pep booted the football against them and, in doing so, experienced that magical moment that occurs when foot contacts leather.

'It's a virus, a virus that's in his blood. It's the football virus,' his mother explained to me as she reminisced about Pep's

early years in her dining room while his father Valentí, a retired bricklayer and extremely industrious man, allowed his gaze to wander over the many trophies and pieces of memorabilia he had collected throughout his son's career. The foreign-language edition of the book you now hold in your hands was also there: *El Método Guardiola.*

Pep Guardiola. The Philosophy That Changed the Game analyses the values that led to Pep Guardiola's becoming the world's best club coach. These are the values of the man who also inspired the Spanish national team's playing style and evoked worldwide admiration for his leadership of such extraordinary (and unique) players as Lionel Messi, Xavi Hernàndez and Andrés Iniesta. These are the values that guarantee exquisite football.

The former FC Barcelona coach's decision to sign a contract with FC Bayern München in December of 2012 was a major success for German football. As proven by winning the triple, FC Bayern has demonstrated impressive results at football's top echelon under the excellent leadership of coach Jupp Heynckes.

Now it's time to answer the one-million-pound question: How can Guardiola not only compete with Jupp Heynckes' legacy but also improve upon it? What is Pep really capable of?

Allow me to make a few comments in this regard.

1. When should a team introduce profound changes? When does this help, and when does it go wrong?

Here we are obviously reminded of the saying, 'Never change a winning team.' However, we also say 'No guts, no glory.' In the end, it is always a question of finding the right combination of conservative, cautious and risky courses of action.

Since time immemorial, wise people have analysed this question but have failed to reach a satisfactory answer. However, one thing has remained constant. A lack of success means time to change. In this instance, there is simply no other choice. As a rule, people stick to what they know when things are going well, but history shows (especially in football) that past performance does not guarantee future success. Football is and remains a game of chance.

The key will be whether Guardiola can maintain the Munich side's motivation. Would Heynckes himself even have been capable of this? Would he even have been capable of motivating himself after winning the triple? Would things have only gone downhill? Who knows…

It's not the worst thing that could happen to successful players who have just won the triple to have to gain the confidence of a new coach. The whole squad will have to show what it is capable of in this season to win the favour of Pep. Not a bad starting point.

2. Every opportunity, many risks

In Spain they say that opportunities are like flies. They are everywhere in the air, but it is almost impossible to catch them. In late 2012, Pep Guariola was 42 years old and living in New York. However, he missed his true love: football! Then an opportunity arose that simply had to be taken. The time had come! Jupp Heynckes (almost 70) was on the finishing straight of his career, and he himself had described Pep Guardiola as his ideal successor.

Uli Hoeneß and the other Bayern managers saw signing Pep after the 2012-2013 season as an enormous opportunity, but they were also aware of the risk.

The topic of Heynckes' future was still on the table, and Guradiola's signing did not present the most favourable conditions for the deserving football master.

I do not know Heynckes personally, but my intuition tells me that he would recognize Pep as the brilliant coach that he is. He could be an excellent mentor to Pep Guardiola and support him in his first months with FC Bayern. Guardiola has a deep respect for people who take logical thinking to its maximum. Heynckes is such a person, a true master of logic and discipline. Guardiola's biography demonstrates that he is prepared to listen to mentors and teachers that he respects. There is an opportunity here, buzzing about like a fly. One must only know how to catch it.

3. What added value can Pep bring?

Pep will naturally be judged by the titles he wins. A championship win would be the minimum expected of him. But what about the DFB Cup? What about the Champions League? That is the sort of pressure that Guardiola knows already from his time with Barça.

If Bayern's leadership gives Pep free reign (including the power to sign players), the squad may improve even more.

In addition to variable tactics, Guardiola can teach the Bavarians aesthetically pleasing football. However, of primary importance will be maintaining the motivation of 2012-2013 in the coming season.

At any rate, if the squad achieves consolidation, it could mean the dawn of a veritable Belle Epoque of Bavarian football to endure for many years to come.

For this reason, Guardiola must be fully integrated into the club's operations. His charisma here is crucial. However, the grounding that he receives in his personal life through his partner Cristina and his three children (Maria, Marius and Valentina) is also decisive. He also maintains constant contact with this parents and grandparents via Skype. If he manages to arrive in Munich and set up his life there, he will also have increased opportunities for success.

It goes without saying that he will also bring the superb football training he received in Barcelona with him to

the Bavarian capital. This training stands for innovative capability and know-how. He can also teach the Bavarians simplicity and elegance as well as one more thing: fair play.

Guardiola believes in celebrating victories with humility, especially when his opponents are arrogant.

If all of these arguments in favour of Guardiola are not enough for you, you have to ask yourself: Does the international market offer any alternative whatsoever? A coach who could decently train the Bavarian team?

4.   Should Guardiola fail…

Football is and remains a contest. Results are what count, and that should never be forgotten. The intense competition on the national and international levels will not forgive Munich any miscalculations. Bayern is distinguished by the fact that it has often won in the last minute. However, the flip side of that is that they have often had victory snatched from them in the very last minute. The situation with Pep appears similar. If he is very lucky, he could be successful, but he could also fall short if his luck fails him.

So what happens if Pep fails?

If Pep fails, he will briefly succumb to his anguish but will return quickly to the calm composure he is known for. Dignity is of the utmost importance to him in this regard. Loyalty is his top priority. He signed a contract. His closest friends also stress this. He would want to fulfil his contract even if he were less successful.

But what does Pep do if he is successful? He will fulfil his contract up through 2016 but will probably not extend it. He will probably take another year-long sabbatical and then aim for a position in the Premier League. This will not be out of contempt for Bayern but the result of his deep-seated drive to broaden his horizons and continuously reinvent himself. Guardiola is always looking for more.

It is what it is. However, even if Pep does become a globetrotter, there is one thing he will remain in his heart of hearts: a proud Catalan.

Guardiola has it in him to combine traditional German virtues, such as high personal expectations, team unity and strong dedication with his southern creativity. We can already congratulate the Bundesliga on gaining such a coach.

We should consider ourselves fortunate as well. We followed and admired Pep during his long tenure with FC Barcelona. This is a club that showed us the best football in the world—football that was ethical and aesthetically pleasing; football that drew on blue-red traditions of past decades (with influences including Rinus Michels, Johan Cruyff and Frank Rijkaard) but was also innovative and bold. It was a playing style based on ball possession, a ball continuously in motion, constant pressure to capture the ball, close cooperation between various team members and defenders that play offense and strikers that play defence. This was football that admirably combined the outstanding abilities of some with a maximum of team play. It was a true beehive of activity, in which Lionel Messi was the queen and the game was pure honey (from now on Brasilian Neymar is the queen bee in petto).

The book that you are holding was published in 2010 with the purpose of answering a question: What is Guardiola's secret to success? The answer: In addition to talented players and outstanding general conditions, it is his special qualities that influence leadership. These are values such as self-sacrifice, humility and commitment, which have continuously waned in importance over recent decades in Catalan and Spanish society. These are values that transfer perfectly from the football pitch to other areas of life, such as business, politics, daily life or family.

All of my predictions have proven true. One by one, the successes I had projected became reality.

The role I predicted for Guardiola as a role model for Catalan society was confirmed by the unanimous support for the honour bestowed upon him by the Parliament of Catalonia. I was also correct, when, to the surprise of many, I expressed my belief that he would leave FC Barcelona after four years as coach. My prediction that he would spend his year on sabbatical in New York also came true. Even his signing with FC Bayern that I (one of the very few) steadfastly believed would happen became reality.

All of these accurate projections have earned me the nickname 'guardiologist' in many journalistic circles. It is a title I bear with pride.

Perhaps Wikipedia could someday define the term Guardiologist as follows:

'Guardiologist: a multidisciplinary analyst, describes the character and behaviour of former FC Barcelona player and coach Josep Guardiola i Sala for the purpose of explaining the influence that Guardiola has on athletics, society and the economy through the enormous popularity of football.'

However, I would like to point out that all of the musings and thoughts found in this book are my own independent assessments. (Oddly enough, I was actually born on the same day of the year as Pep Guardiola, January 18.) They are based on my own analyses and conversations with people close to Pep. They in no way reflect official or authorised points of view. I take full responsibility for both correct and false statements.

Although it may change in Germany, it is common knowledge that Pep Guardiola has not granted any interviews thus far even though he is prepared to answer any question imaginable during press conferences. I took full advantage of this when I participated in Guardiola's press conferences as a journalist (a profession I pursued for many decades).

The whole world knows that the former Barcelona coach is very concerned with protecting his privacy. At the same time, in light of the media's great influence, he also pays meticulous attention to his public image. In this context, there are people who accuse him of false humility, hypocrisy, dissimulation and false egocentricity. He has also been accused of exploiting others; being deceitful, excessive, compulsive and moody; and having preferences and aversions in dealing with people.

Are these things true? In this situation, we should remember the words of the poet regarding truth. These things are a mirror broken into a thousand pieces. Each individual shard represents a piece of the truth.

It is extremely difficult to know a person fully. It is hard enough to know oneself, and it is all the more complicated to speculate about the spiritual lives of others. However, there do exist reliable benchmarks: behaviour and results. In this case, the balance of Guardiola's extraordinary professional results, deserving of admiration and respect, is revealed to be far beyond any sports rivalry and unfounded commentary.

It is naturally difficult to believe that Guardiola will be able to reproduce the unbelievable successes with FC Bayern that he celebrated in Barcelona. The Guardiola era coincided with a unique generation of players that had trained and matured at La Masía and internalised the same playing style and admirable athletic values of camaraderie and fairness. These were the youth academy trademarks that Guardiola also has in his veins.

Of course, it did not escape anyone that Guardiola was responsible for signing several players in his successful period who put the club in difficult financial straits. On the other hand, he promoted the club's own talents with courage and tenacity and forged a team of primarily home-grown champions of which the club's supporters were especially proud. However, it will take time, at least a decade, for the La Masía youth academy to form another generation such as this.

The FC Bayern München team offers Pep Guardiola a wonderful opportunity to demonstrate his qualities as a coach within the framework of one of the most efficient sports organisations in existence. It is a chance born out of an intimate connection between southern creativity and German engineering that could produce a benchmark-setting team in Europe. This could be the continuation the Belle Époque that Heynckes started by winning the triple.

Bayern has very high demands, but Pep's abilities are also extraordinary. Moreover, the philosophy and values of both sides are similar. The passion that Guardiola devotes to the task at hand will soon be recognised in Bavaria, and the results will stem from this. Football is not a science. It is above all an art. Guardiola possesses both art and method.

Guardiola is workhorse. He is studying German almost obsessively. After signing the contract, he began learning German six months before his arrival in Munich. He works with a German instructor four hours a day and does additional exercises in the language of Goethe during his free time.

There is one obvious explanation for this: Guardiola wants to become a member of society in Munich and in Germany. He knows the importance of language to a culture. Without the language, he would not be able to truly understand and become acquainted with his environment. Without this understanding, Guardiola could not do his job successfully.

He also knows that he will be under constant observation. His successor, Tito Vilanova, will be compared to Guardiola step by step in Barcelona and throughout Spain.

I am excited about this challenge. I absolutely want to experience it first hand and will occasionally leave my home for Munich, a city where I already lived in in the 1980s as a student. I also lived in Heidelberg, Bremen and West Berlin. By the way, I also spent 12 years living on the heavenly island of Mallorca just 50 metres from the Bierstraße (beer street) on Playa de Palma beach.

I hope that I will soon be able to make presentations based on my book in German just as I have done many times in Spanish throughout Spain and in English when visiting places abroad where Pep Guardiola (and FC Barcelona) garners an extremely high level of respect.

Pep's influence could also lead to an evolution and a reassessment of the German language in Spain.

The Goethe Cabinet, a group of Spanish-German cohabitation analysts that I chair (consisting of managers, specialists and Goethe Institute instructors), has observed that Pep has done a lot in this regard. He is demonstrating that language learning promotes cultural understanding of other countries and the importance of that understanding. This is a major opportunity.

With this transition, the Bavarian capital will also become the capital of guardiology, the multidiscipline analysis of Pep Guardiola's personality. I have no doubt that the Pep experience has a clear expiration date. It will be an intense period even if it is relatively short (presumably four years). Prepare yourself for a hyperactive, charismatic and nonconformist man—a great persuader. He is an energetic and even sensitive and meticulous person who will also soon enter German society as a popular role model.

He is a coach who will probably return to FC Barcelona someday. However, he will not go back as a coach but as a top leader in sports. That means he will be club president, and in doing so, he will fulfil the FC Bayern tradition of great former players taking on leadership positions.

He would become the 'Catalan Beckenbauer.' He possesses his own style and is a well-read and highly-educated person with a many-faceted, ever-changing state of mind, great ambitions and a desire to anticipate everything. He is radical in his indulgences and a perfectionist to the point of compulsion. He has an exceedingly great and restless heart. His father's description of him is succinct: He is 'a good person.'

But first things first. Now it is time for you to enjoy Pep Guardiola and shed tears with him—tears of joy of course.

Barcelona, 21 April 2013, two days before the Champions League Semi-final between FC Bayern München and FC Barcelona

and

Barcelona, 17 June 2013, one week before Guardiola's first press conference in Munich's Allianz Arena.

Miguel Angel Violán

Follow the author on Twitter: @maviolan

THE ESTEEMED

PEP GUARDIOLA

THE ESTEEMED
PEP GUARDIOLA ■ ■ ■

(FOREWORD TO THE SECOND CATALAN EDITION)

I was a happy man on 8 September 2011. That was the day when the Parliament of Catalonia bestowed the Gold Medal on Barça coach Josep Guardiola i Sala, and the lad from Santpedor became an official role model for the people of Catalonia today. That was exactly the thesis I had presented in my book *Pep Guardiola: His Method*, published a year earlier after finishing it in Boston in May of 2010.

Equipped with my press pass, I entered the main parliament session chamber and initially stood towards the back of the room between the audience and photographers. I didn't miss a single detail of the ceremony, especially Pep's speech that would draw so much attention.

When the ceremony was over, I broke every protocol rule in the book and broke through the right-hand side of the outside ring with the youthful vigour of a Cuenca or a Tello (two major talents in Catalan youth football). I approached Pep's mother, who was still in a wheelchair at that time because of a fall, and said to her:

'My father was a bricklayer just like your husband. My mother's name is Dolores just like yours. And I was born on January 18 like Pep. Could you tell me the time of day when he was born?' She gave me an astonished and amused look and said to me very motherly:

'Around one o'clock.'

'a.m.?'

'No, p.m.'

Mission accomplished. I was satisfied. I had found out that the young and successful FC Barcelona coach who had asked the nation to 'get up early, very early' had come into the world later in the day than I had. (I was born at six o'clock in the morning).

Several months later in Pep's parents' dining room in Santpedor, I reminded her of this anecdote as she recounted various details of her highly decorated son's childhood.

That day, the 8th of September, I left the Catalan parliament building firmly convinced that I had heard the second most important speech of my life. Most important was the commencement address at Stanford University given by Apple founder Steve Jobs who unfortunately passed away one month after Pep's award ceremony. Jobs' speech may not have attracted as much attention, but it was full of great messages and impressive statements. This applies primarily to Jobs' references to the brevity of our existence

('Death is very likely the single best invention of life.'), our unavoidable demise and the necessity of identifying with death to gain inspiration and cherish our passing with heart and soul.

I realized that Pep's speech before parliament was actually a lecture on his method, the Guardiola method. It was a description of the values and convictions that had made the Catalan the best coach in the world at just over 40 and a role model for a large portion of a Catalan society feeling disoriented and frustrated in turbulent times.

It was a society confronted with two types of bankruptcy: financial and moral.

ADDICTED TO SPEECHES AND LECTURES

I have devoted 35 years of my life to journalism and the art of communication in general. For over a decade, I have been training public speakers as a university lecturer and working with professionals in the field of communication. Around 4,000 people have attended my courses and seminars at the Colegio de Periodistas de Cataluña, and I have had the privilege of training approximately 10,000 in my lectures throughout Spain. There were a good 500 attendees at my beloved Centro Superior de Hostelería de Galicia and a good handful at the University of Oviedo, Instituto de Empresa University in Madrid, EAE Business School and Universitat Internacional de Catalunya.

In doing this, I have become a specialist in the art of public speaking. The analysis of speeches and forms of expression used by leaders is actually one of my favourite areas of research. If I were to describe this in Guardiola's words, I would say that language inspires me and that I am a 'fiery supporter' of speeches as long as they have substance and communicate emotions as Pep did with his speech in the semicircle of the Catalan parliament.

I have taken the liberty of dissecting the speech made on 8 September 2011. I have analysed some things as a researcher and of others as a guardiologist. I formed this neologism along with my admirable colleague Dani Sanabre. It was part of my contribution to his radio programme *Tu diràs* on RAC1 as we attempted to filter out Guardiola's messages from his cryptic press conference statements regarding his contract extension.

This was the source of the term *duty Guardiologist,* meaning a so-called specialist who attempts to deduce what Pep really wants to say (no easy task, when Pep himself intentionally avoids using clear-cut statements) by analysing clues and associated communicative factors such as gestures and ambiguous statements.

It goes without saying that I also followed his press conferences either from home or by attending them personally. When present at these events, I would always take advantage of the privilege of being allowed to ask one question. Now that is no longer possible. At that time,

I enjoyed it thoroughly and was able to gather important information for this book.

My examination of the speech by the *Muy Honorable Pep* meaning *Most Honourable Pep* (a title traditionally reserved for the president or the *Generalitat* (the entirety of Catalonia's autonomous institutions), which I have taken the liberty of borrowing) was a fun and *continuously fascinating* experience for me.

My university students know this very well as we carried out a comprehensive analysis of Pep's 10-minute speech. As we worked, each discovery was a magic moment. It might not be sufficient justification for the creation of an entire career field, but it is definitely ample grounds for many hours of self-induced seclusion and careful analysis. As Steve Jobs, who had been to death's door and back again in 2005, so aptly put it, 'Do what you love and love what you do.' And as we work, we should display the same passion as Pep Guardiola constantly demands.

The 10 Points of the Guardiola Method

1. As psychologist and my friend Antoni Bolinches very aptly put it, a method consists of both attitudes and preferences.

2. Have the courage to have values. He took this phrase out of my book (without my knowledge). Nike subsequently printed this exact phrase on their FC Barcelona players' jersey.

3. The values of Pep's Barça can be applied to any type of organisation. Ultimately, every organisation has to have people. (By the way, Banco Sabadell designed a well-known advertising campaign based on the concept of my book, which I had handed to a member of its board of directors on the train from Barcelona to Madrid.)

4. An organisation (or company, country or society) is always to be viewed as type of subjective condition.

5. A happy cow produces more milk (which was actually proven by the admirable La Fageda dairy cooperative in Garrotxa). The same applies to people. There is nothing better than having content and motivated people at one's disposal.

6. Success also always has something to do with a team, because commonly shared intelligence produces synergies and multiplies the value of the outstanding abilities of individuals.

7. Play as you train. If we strive for perfection, we must hone every component on a daily basis; always expect maximum effort from ourselves, and recognise good work when we see it.

8. Knowledge cannot be imparted without respect. This is why universities in the field of economics should also return to the values that made them big (as they say in the U.S., 'Get back to their roots.'). The widespread *Urdangarinisation* (derived from Juahi Urdangarin,

stepson of the King of Spain and the legal proceedings involving accusations of embezzlement and gross tax evasion associated with him) of recent years has created the need for a deep clean, vermin extermination and an adjustment and replacement of leadership. This should be carried out in a way that allows the voices of both university graduates and the so-called stakeholders, the people directly affected, to be heard.

9. If Barça is more than a football club, then Guardiola is more than a mere coach.

10. Healthy common sense is the essence of the whole concept and the cornerstone of the leadership model practiced by Guardiola. It is this healthy level of common sense that enables leaders that possess it (like Pep) to achieve extraordinary results.

NOW WHAT IS COMMON SENSE?

I would like to propose a very precise and understandable definition of the term *healthy common sense,* which has been interpreted countless times both philosophically and semantically. *Common sense* is the ability to think of those around us. The word *sense* refers to the capacity for contemplation, while *common* relates to society and our social environment. How many times have misfortunes and disasters resulted from the isolated decisions of economic powers and their reckless leaders? These decisions were made possible through the development of the capitalist

system against all common sense and in total disregard for
people and human dignity.

This was the source of my feelings of indignation (even if
I was not the first to use this term in this context) when I
wrote about analysing contemporary Catalan society in the
previous editions. Catalan society is constantly subjected
to heavy criticism, and I would like to juxtapose it with a
model of virtuosity that I call the *6:2 generation*. These
are young and uninhibited people, in the good sense of
the word, that have perfect training and are anything
but defeatist. They are the ones who had the privilege
of experiencing that fantastic 6:2 victory over Barça's
greatest rival Real Madrid in Santiago Bernabéu Stadium
during Pep Guardiola's first year.

The obvious lack of healthy common sense brought to light by the current world crisis has shown me how important it is to strengthen social cooperation and find the courage to share with others those things that stand in opposition to blind and senseless ambition.

AN ODE TO DOLPHINS

Oddly enough, I discovered the unambiguous advantages of harmonious coexistence by working with dolphins. I have had the privilege of participating in research (some of which occurred in the United States) with these extraordinarily intelligent marine mammals. Dolphins demonstrate the sensitive sort of intelligence that at times seems more human than that of humans. They have developed a capacity for adaptation that has enabled them (thus far) to survive as a species. They practice hedonism, sensual pleasure (including self-gratification) and possess a comprehensive self-image and the physical and psychological capacity to induce their own death. They commit suicide (here I am referring to the monumental and gripping documentary film *The Cove*). I have the feeling that "animal" intelligence, in all of its nuances, could in many ways be beneficial to us in designing the organisations of the 21st century in a more humane manner.

I had a fascinating experience swimming with dolphins on Mexico's Yucatán Peninsula in 1997. As I was about to pet one of the dolphins, I noticed that a female had approached a woman in our group and was nuzzling her stomach.

The waterpark trainer said,

'Congratulations! You're pregnant!'

The surprised woman replied,

'That's true, for a few months now. But how did the dolphin know that?'

The explanation astounded me. Dolphins transmit sound waves and scan their environment in order to understand the objects around them. In this case, the female dolphin had, in a manner of speaking, taken an ultrasound of the woman's abdomen. However, I was most surprised by the dolphin's compassionate reaction, the ability to put itsel in another's shoes and caress the tiny person growing in the woman's womb in a display of motherly affection.

This experience made a tremendous impression on me, and it still seems as if it happened only yesterday. I would be very interested in further researching these animals' sensitive and compassionate intelligence.

SENSITIVE INTELLIGENCE

Let's return to Pep Guardiola. Just as with dolphins, intelligence and sensibility are the attributes that characterise him best. However, Pep also has a third attribute: coherence.

FC Barcelona Foundation vice president Gabriel Masfurroll used these three traits in describing Guardiola. The many hours that I have spent in conversation with people close to Pep have also provided a categorical confirmation of this.

The traits mentioned cannot be used to describe Jose Mourinho, Guardiola's greatest opponent on the football pitch. To put it quite bluntly, I believe that lines such as 'The end justifies the means' or 'victory at all costs' are more representative of Mourinho's philosophy. There have been a number of instances in which the Portuguese coach has given inaccurate analyses and provided for excursions in the field of psychiatry with his behaviour, which, from a purely legal standpoint, have tested the boundaries of criminal conduct multiple times. Backed by influential individuals, he has continually set an example of irresponsibility and lack of sportsmanship.

Episodes such as Mourinho's poking FC Barcelona assistant coach Tito Vilanov in the eye, the unpunished aggression Real Madrid's Pepe against Messi, insults, vulgar gestures and constant manipulation of information have turned the Madrid team into moral losers regardless of their results on the pitch. This all stands in stark contrast to the traditional values that made the royals so powerful in the past and helped them leverage the support of millions. Many of these people are now looking to Barça.

I do not want to conclude this chapter of the book without mentioning the numerous magic moments that we had the privilege of experiencing in recent years. The experience of broadcasting the Guardiola message to all of the cities and villages of Catalonia, throughout Spain and many countries abroad (including *the Real Colegio Complutense* at Harvard

University) was something that I cannot overestimate. I often had the feeling of becoming a medium for external and extremely positive emotions, as many people would show affection to me as Pep Guardiola's ambassador. I am very thankful for this role as an intermediary. It was a wonderful experience and a gift of fate.

I would especially like to mention the two years of the *El mètodo Guardiola: valors en joc (The Guardiola Method: Values at Play)* programme on Ràdio Estel created in close cooperation with Toni Huguet, Mario Ramírez, my favourite editors (whom we christened "the unstoppables"), the versatile midfielders in production, Blanca Aranyó, Marta Cruz (also an excellent photographer) and Laia Garcia (an up-and-coming vocal artist). We had a lot of fun together and did some good work. I would like to highlight the programme's theme song created by songwriter Ivan Rosquellas. I already had the opportunity of collaborating with him on the *El Suplement* programme on Catalunya Ràdio. Everything was seamless. Incidentally, I have taken the liberty of enclosing the Catalan text based on *The Guardiola Method* and the music of "Viva la Vida" with this book. The latter is the Coldplay title track that Pep Guardiola used to motivate his team in his first few seasons.

I would also like to say a special word of thanks to all of the guests of the programme, including FC Barcelona president Agustí Montal; FC Barcelona youth football coordinator and author of *La força d'un somni (The Power of a Dream)* Albert Puig; entrepreneur Gabriel Masfurroll; doctor, dream specialist and great communicator Eduard

Estivill; and former Barcelona mayor Jordi Hereu, a politician of remarkable sensitivity. I have especially fond memories of Joan Nogués, a Catalan language teacher who recited the poems of Miquel Martí i Pol in such an impressive manner. His eye-winking undertone is entirely to the taste of Pep Guardiola.

I hold in my memory the awe-inspiring oral fluency of publicist Joaquín Lorente, the articles by former FC Barcelona presidential candidate Agustí Benedito, the academic excursions of professor Francesc Torralba, the poetic power of Joan Margarit, and the balanced considerations of Fabricio Caivano, Spanish National Journalism Prize laureate and former director of the renowned *Cuadernos de Pedagogía* newspaper.

A SAD NOTE

There is also a sad event that must be noted. My father passed away in Barcelona on 27 November 2011. Enric Violán i Tohà, who suffered from Alzheimer's disease and other illnesses was the focus of our concerns over the past five years (the same time as Guardiola's Barça era) and was the reason that I moved back to Barcelona from Mallorca. I had spent 12 years on the island as the communications director for the Riu Hotels & Resorts chain.

My father's ashes now rest in a *finca* (Spanish rural hom)] on the edge of the village of Vidrà in the Catalan county of Ripollès, to which he dedicated a good portion of his 83 years. Two young trees stand in memory of the fact that he

once worked there and that he is no longer with us. From my father, I inherited my proclivity for wordplays and my sometimes-obsessive penchant for creative chaos. That also goes for my intermittent, unexplainably phlegmatic and at times somewhat self-conscious temperament, my inclination to avoid things interspersed with a deep curiosity that always returns and sporadically reveals itself and my endeavour to establish a country deep inside where there is room for just one citizen: me.

And another comment: I would also like to express my gratitude for the constant support of former FC Barcelona vice president Evarist Murtra. To me, his speech before the Catalan Parliament is on the same level as the well-placed and valuable words of writer David Trueba, a close friend of Pep Guardiola.

Evarist and I presented this book at the Barcelona Bar Association together as well as at the Association of Catalan Journalists a year later. We did the second presentation along with sports journalist Dani Senabre whose talent and spontaneity captivate me although he is shamelessly young. We share a common passion: Boston.

It is an honour to have Murtra's support. I do not know what he saw in me that moved him to give me his trust or what caused him to honour me in this way. I am fully aware of the privilege I enjoy as well as the responsibility to not take his friendship for granted. In these times, such friendship is a rare and therefore even more precious asset. Evarist, thank you for your wisdom!

GOOD TIMES FOR GOOD PEOPLE

At one of my latest public appearances, as I was speaking about the Guardiola method in view of the value of leadership qualities and coaching techniques, the following subtitle occurred to me: *How can one become better when everything is becoming worse?*

I was still in mourning for my father and felt the need to broadcast a message of comfort regarding coaching. I had recently become involved in this activity following my first inspiring experience with world motorcycling champion Jorge Lorenzo.

In my view, improvement of self and others is the most noble of all activities. In these rough and difficult times, this is the very hour when we must stand up and explore our own full potential.

As the last point of my introduction, I would like to say that I believe in the notion that great crises offer great opportunities for improvement. That is why I take the liberty of predicting, without wanting to sound naive, that good times are ahead. It simply must be so. Good times for good people.

In any case, I feel a strong obligation to ensure this very thing, both as a writer who teaches and as a teacher who writes. I'll say it once more so everyone can take note of it:

Good times for good people.
'The joy one gives to others lasts the longest.'
(Antoni Bolinches)

"HAVE THE COURAGE

TO HAVE VALUES"

"HAVE THE COURAGE TO HAVE VALUES" ■ ■ ■

THE BLUE-RED SOUL—BY EVARIST MURTRA[1]

In the back of my mind I always have the words of FC Barcelona president Narcís de Carreras (a man of integration) that he spoke during very difficult times in 1969.

'We must fight against everything and against the whole world. We are the best, and we represent what we are.'

Represent. A sacred term. We act on behalf of others. We represent them. We owe them something and must serve them with body and soul. We represent them and want the best for them.

This is the only way that true affection for an institution can be understood. FC Barcelona is an institution of enormous social significance. It is more than a mere football club.

The institution itself was founded by Joan Gamper, a citizen of Switzerland. It was an initiative born out social values with a clear acknowledgement of pluralism and

---

[1] Former FC Barcelona vice president

respect for diversity. The wins and athletic glory came next, in that exact order. This is why it is impossible to imagine social values being placed above results on the pitch at FC Barcelona. 'Sport and citizenship', as our President, the martyr Josep Sunyol i Garriga, said. He was murdered at the outset of the Spanish Civil War in 1936.

It must be understood why this is so. Success in sports comes and goes. What doesn't work one day can be effective the next. That is how things are in sports. The current situation and other circumstances have an influence, and of course it also has something to do with luck.

However, it was precisely the act of defending citizens' rights that led to the club's founding, and it was this factor that would produce the desired success in the game sooner or later. It is what makes us strong in difficult times and proud in times of victory. And everything originates from one single, unshakeable principle: a close bond between the people and their club. The support of the nation. This is precisely what enables us to be successful and rise above ourselves.

The history of FC Barcelona is long and focuses the people who played a role in it. The presidential terms in office are fragments of the club's history. They are definitely part of the club's history, but also only fragments of it. The institution itself remains. It does not disappear. It survives us and will still be there when our time has passed.

For this reason, we must have the utmost respect and total affection for this history over our personal egoism. Ultimately, it represents us all.

We are only ever as strong as our values. It is not enough to merely achieve good results on the pitch. The hopes and dreams of the blue-red nation are also characterised by these values. This could also be seen in the results of the last FC Barcelona presidential election in June of 2010 when the spokesman of the status quo failed miserably.

How can such results be explained after seven years of game successes, a period marked by manifest improvements in the club's financial situation and improved solidarity through the FC Barcelona foundation?

There is no other explanation than the former president's poor leadership. Joan Laporta did not represent the institution well. He did not serve the individual members of the club. He broadened the gaps between the various factions and represented none of the values that made the club so strong in the past.

He displayed exaggerated self-esteem in the performance of his duties and arrogance and a lack of generosity when the time came to share successes with his comrades-in-arms. His blunt way of expressing true FC Barcelona qualities like the indispensable Catalan character was not accompanied by the necessary humility and elegance.

The former president's accomplishments are in fact truly remarkable in sporting terms. However, he fell short when it came to the values of the people and the club's members.

With time, Barça supporters will come to view him as an important person in the areas I have mentioned, the areas that he promoted during his tenure in office.

It was none other than Pep Guardiola who showed us that values are of significant importance in life. His success would be unthinkable without his values.

Pep combines the virtues and values of many people who came before him. Would it be possible to understand a Pep Guardiola without an Oriol Tort who has been responsible for the youth academy since the 1970s? Or without the great Johan Cruyff under the presidency of Agustí Montal? Without the chance that president Núñez gave him to coach the team in the late 1980s?

Can the Dream Team be understood without first mentioning Carles Reixach?

It is unlikely that there is a veteran FC Barcelona supporter out there who does not recognise certain similarities between the legendary Samitier and Pep himself.

Pep has inherited a little from all of these personalities. He has assimilated them and put one principal first in doing so—the love for Barça is most important of all.

Now I would like to mention one of the initiatives that has made a very special contribution to the institution's prestige in recent years: its support of UNICEF.

Via UNICEF, we offer the means to improve the future of children who have the least. It is an honour for us both as an institution and as human beings. It is an attempt to show the wealthy global football community that, in a little corner of this planet, there is a Catalan club that is one of the best in the world and wants to give back a little of what it has achieved by giving to the children.

There is nothing finer for a Barcelona supporter than seeing a child playing football in a blue-red jersey in a country that is not developed enough to ensure at least a minimum standard of living.

UNICEF is a means of achieving this but not the objective in itself. If this were so, it would be a hypocritical venture serving as a mere marketing campaign and to clear our conscience. Fortunately, the club's foundation launched highly commendable initiatives in this regard during President Joan Laporta's tenure. If there were one thing to criticise, it would be the fact that the project did not resonate sufficiently in the media and people did not hear about it.

The book that you hold analyses Pep's values. It is a careful analysis and the result of observations and document studying. Its aim is to understand Pep and to find out how he has managed to apply this combination of talent and dedication in a sport with the greatest competitive pressure worldwide.

The author made a tremendous effort and put more emphasis on the values themselves that on the results achieved. As Miguel Angel Violán has already said, one must first 'Have the courage to have values.' This includes the knowledge that one is serving others with coherence and decency, which, in itself is the definition of common sense as the author understands it.

It is these social values that bestow true greatness upon us. As a purebred professional in the service of FC Barcelona, Pep Guardiola embodies these values more than any other.

Institutions also have a soul. The blue-red soul is composed of a love for sports (football above all), but it also includes social values such as a fighting spirit, sense of responsibility, respect, honesty and teamwork. Pep receives a top score not only in terms of success on the pitch but also when it comes to these values.

Barça fans have fully recognised this, and that is why we all love him.

The great challenge for the new generation of Barcelonistas is to continue winning on the pitch and in doing so, to serve the people at all times. All of this measures up to the role model provided by Pep. We must be very clear about our roots and also know that 'we represent what we are.'

This is underscored above all by the speeches given by Evarist Murtra and Pep Guardiola before the Parliament of Catalonia. It is the reason why we are printing all of this.

SPEECH BY EVARIST MURTRA, FORMER FC BARCELONA VICE PRESIDENT, BEFORE THE PARLIAMENT OF CATELONIA

It is a special honour for me to be able to say a few words about a friend who is especially close to my heart: Josep Guardiola i Sala. He has become an absolute role model for others, not only because of the success he has achieved in sports but also for the way in which he has done it.

However, please allow me first to read a few words by director, journalist and screenwriter David Trueba, a good friend of the person we are here to honour. The organisers invited him to be here today as well, but he was unfortunately unable to attend due to professional obligations. When I learned that he would not be able to attend, I proposed that he dedicate a few words to Pep. I believe they describe very well the person who has brought us here today.

THE WORDS OF DAVID TRUEBA

First of all, I would like to thank Evarist for giving me this backdoor opportunity to participate in honouring Pep. It is a shame that I cannot be with you as there are very few opportunities to say something publically about this person who is so close to my heart. Incidentally, I believe the fact that a *Madrileno* (native of Madrid) is present at this occasion in Pep's honour gives us a few indications about his personality.

The essence of Pep lies in the fact that he is a footballer who was not satisfied with mere sporting success and fame. He always sought out the people in his world who could give him something. I can think of no better definition of friendship. It characterises your career, your family, the generation to which you belong, your homeland and your own preferences. Friends are a valuable luxury. They help you repair your gutters when you have cracks in your roof. They remind you that not everyone has it as good as you. They force you to face the things that you have long ignored because you were only looking at yourself. They share your obsessions, your disappointments and your dreams. By doing so, they give you a piece of someone else. Sharing friendship with another means sharing their fate as part of your own. This is how Pep has managed to make it so that many who view football sceptically or only from a distance see this world of Barcelona as their own personal challenge. He treats football with so much tenderness and love that one is forced to see this sport as more than just a business. It is an irrational passion or an exhibition of football artistry.

The team that Pep leads best is his friends. They are devoted to him and go where their chief tactician wants them. Everyone should hold to his virtues. They assure protection of one's weak points.

You have been through calm and stormy seas. That ever so pleasant pat on the shoulder and the applause are not always there, but these moments of calm have shown you who your true friends are.

I know that you know that an absolute condition for being honoured is being convinced that you do not deserve it. That is why the only reason you came today was to give your parents some measure of pride. I would like to thank them for making you into what you are. This especially goes for your mother, for all of the times that she took the ball away from you. Many of us would never have had the pleasure of getting to know you if you had not noticed that there are other things in the world besides kicking the ball. And even though the game of football and your players are what brought you here to be honoured today, it is your playing off the pitch that gives you the special quality that people value in you so very much.

As a friend and football illiterate, I can only tell you that there will always be a cool bottle of Cava waiting for you at my home whenever you want to come by, whether you've won or lost and whether you're sick or well.

I congratulate you on being who you are. That is the greatest accomplishment of all. Thank you and give my very best regards to everyone!

– David Trueba

I would also like to speak about him, about my young friend who was an excellent player in his time and, at just 40 years old, still has so much ahead of him although he has already become a role model for many.

I met Pep Guardiola in early 2003. It was not long before Barça's presidential elections, and he had put his name on the list to become Lluís Bassat's technical secretary. We considered it appropriate that we get to know one another and found an opportunity for this in the city of Brescia.

I took an important insight home with me from this journey. Pep is a well-bred person who radiates something that used to be a separate subject in school in the past:

decency and ethics. He received his good upbringing by being raised in a home characterised by human values: the Guardiola i Sala family from the village of Santpedor. Dolores and Valentí planted the seed. Pep cultivated it further in his time at FC Barcelona's La Masía youth academy. There he was brought up in a spirit that made him fight every day to improve a little bit more.

I realised that, even though we were far from home, he was up-to-date about everything happening in Catalonia. He asked incessantly about the latest goings-on, although, as was to be expected, Barça was the most important topic of our conversation.

It really surprised me that he asked me about earlier episodes of the club's history, and that's when I realised that his passion for Barça was much greater than the results of the coming presidential elections.

He captivated me.

A few months later, back in Barcelona, we met with a high-ranking club functionary to learn about Barça's financial situation first hand.

What we had already suspected was then confirmed. The club was in a difficult situation, and a comprehensive reorganisation would be necessary if we were to win the elections.

As we were leaving the room, Pep said to me, *'We cannot directly contact any representatives of other clubs or*

players. That would make future transfers even more costly.
I will not draw my salary until the situation improves.'

That was when I noticed that I had encountered an extraordinary person for whom the end would never justify the means even if it meant us losing the elections. I told him that and he replied, 'I know, but we must not betray the Barça cause.'

It was ultimately Laporta's circle that won the elections in mid-2003. The years went by and Pep became the Barça's B squad coach, which had just dropped into the third league at that time. The young man had returned to his club. He was prepared to serve it as he always had and gain experience in his new position.

I was a member of the club's board of directors at that time and observed how Pep evoked the trust and respect of everyone he worked with: from administrative personnel, to football professionals, to those involved in managing a club as complex as FC Barcelona.

There is really no reason to seek explanations for his rise to the position of coach of the first team. He was selected because he was considered the best option within the club when Txiki Begiristain, the technical secretary at that time, recommended him despite a lack of broad acceptance for him in opinion polls.

And that is how Pep turned out to be the coach of an outstanding team.

It is not easy being the coach of FC Barcelona. Barça has seen over 50 coaches come and go since its founding. So as to remain on track I will not speak here of the many titles he won but rather of the values he imparts and the ultimate reason for his being honoured here today. I mean his sportsmanship, teamwork and willingness to give it his all and to overcome his own limitations. All of this is part of the picture of a cultivated, civilised and cosmopolitan Catalonia that he has helped to create. A well-known phrase that can be read far and wide of late sums this up very well: *'Have the courage to have values.'*

Pep is a privileged man. He is one of the few people that I know who manage to deal with the imperative, important and essential aspects of their personal and professional lives. In a club like Barcelona, it is imperative to win games and titles. It is important to win them with decency and respect for the opponent, as is required in every sport. It is essential to remain loyal to the institution that one represents and maintain the spirit of its founding fathers. Barça is an institution, about which many have come to believe is more than just a club. This is due to its close relationship with the people. 'Sport and citizenship' was the phrase coined by former club president Josep Sunyol i Garriga, who was murdered in the Sierra de Guadarrama Mountains at the outset of the Civil War.

Pep has been an innovator when it comes to sports management. Within days of taking his new position, he had moved the first squad to the club's training ground, the *Ciudad Deportiva.* He surrounded himself with a staff and meticulously planned every detail of each player's training regimen with them. The team was led as a unit, and the youth squad was a crucial element serving the general interest (i.e., the first squad).

These innovations were introduced by a man who could just as easily be described as an entrepreneur.

Like all good entrepreneurs, he has a well-defined sense of justice. That also provides us an indication of how long he will remain with the first team. The most difficult thing for him is setting up a team for a match. He has to decide to bench players who deserve to be regulars in light of their proximity to him, their dedication, their passion and their talent. This is why he suffers. How the group accepts his decisions will determine how long he will remain in this position within the club.

There are entrepreneurs who, for objective reasons, have to deal with redundancies and position reductions at one time or another. Pep does this over 50 times a year (at every game), and if one is profoundly honest, it is difficult to live with these types of decisions despite the fact that they are unavoidable.

Humility is another characteristic that our friend has injected into the entire team. Respect for opponents, temperance in victory and self-criticism when necessary— all of these factors ensure that Barça always radiates something positive in both victory and defeat. For many Barcelona supporters, and I include myself in this, a football match has three halves: the two that everyone knows and a third, the press conference with the coach after the game. Pep's calm, courageous and ever well-mannered bearing engenders confidence at these events.

It is the sum of many things that makes Pep a role model in difficult times such as these. This is especially so in Catalonia where growth and prosperity have historically had their roots in forming associations and pooling resources. This type of cooperation, a social pyramid, has made us strong, great and open to change throughout our history.

I have attempted to dissect his personality, the many good qualities he possesses and the scope of his virtues, which has already reached international proportions.

It is only fitting that we are now also publically recognising the example that he sets.

I take pride in calling him a fellow citizen, and at the same time he is a man admired around the world, a world-class Catalan.

Or quite simply 'Pep', one of us.

If we follow his example, we will only be in the right and no injustice shall befall us.

Thank you.

—Evarist Murtra

PEP GUARDIOLA'S

SPEECH

PEP GUARDIOLA'S
SPEECH ■ ■ ■

BEFORE THE PARLIAMENT OF CATALONIA

'Madam President of Parliament, President of the Generalitat, Mr. Mayor, President of Barça, members of parliament, friends, Dad and Mum.' (0:34)

Formal introduction executed correctly in accordance with protocol—as it should be. Even his parents are mentioned in the salutation. In the beginning, he shows a few signs of nervousness, touches the microphone, and repeatedly says "uhh." Throughout the first minutes, we also hear various false tones.

'This demonstration, thank you Mõnica, is evidence of how much talent this state really has. Evarist, I don't have any idea where you are at the moment, but you were also spot on, just like a tenor trained in a vocal academy. Thank you very much for your effort. I asked you personally to do it and am very happy that you did it. I know that it isn't easy. Nina, thank you for singing that beautiful song by Miquel.' (1:00)

Here he refers to Mònica Terribas, director of Televisión de Cataluña, who had publically praised him and highlighted his healthy common sense and work ethic a few minutes before saying that he "honoured" the society to which he belongs. They have been friends for a very long time. They have been through much together and have many mutual friends.

He refers to former Barça Vice President Evarist Murtra, who is in attendance at the ceremony with his wife. Murtra is the one who signed Guardiola as FC Barcelona's coach. When Pep won his sixth title, Murtra wept openly on the pitch. Guardiola dedicated his success to his friend Evarist Murtra whose mobile phone incidentally died a few seconds after the incident mentioned.

Nina, the singer, had performed a song with lyrics from the poem Solstici by the deceased poet Miquel Martí i Pol just a few minutes before. Martí was Pep's friend, and Pep admired him greatly.

'I asked myself yesterday how important this place is. This place here that also represents all of us. The most important institution of this state. And believe me, it is very important to me. Truly important. I would like to note four things. If praise makes a person weak, my friends, then I am totally destroyed. After everything that has been said about me, I am fumut [pulverised].' (1:23)

Pep is still visibly nervous. However, he already begins combining protocol formality with a somewhat chummy tone, which is also shown by the use of the Catalan term, fumut. He now starts feeling at home in the dialect. He has a small booklet in front of him, in which he as apparently noted some thoughts. It seems to be there more to help him feel at ease than as a memory aid.

'Quite honestly, I would like to simply and plainly say what I feel. I was chosen.' (1:28)

This statement is a sort of turning point for Pep. It is an impressive sentence. He says it with a certain gravity but with no overconfidence whatsoever. He uses the pause as a strategic tool (a useful but difficult-to-implement tool used only by practised public speakers).

From this moment on, he appears to feel at ease. Metaphorically speaking, it is as if he now aware of the field conditions. His messages now come out in fluent succession, and he repeats fundamental terms (for example: 'chosen'). This is a technique called redundancy in public speaking.

'I was chosen. Any other person could have been chosen as the coach of FC Barcelona, but I was chosen. The credit for this goes to the people who made that decision.' (1:38)

It is interesting how the term credit functions in this situation. He calls himself 'chosen' (like a prophet or the hero in the Matrix) but simultaneously demonstrates his humility by giving the credit to others.

'David told me that. He is a very, very good friend of mine and told me that in confidence. On the day that President Laporta and his people believed that I could be the coach of FC Barcelona, he called me and said, "Believe me, the only credit that you have is that you have been chosen." I believe this was a very good approach to this job. Actually it could not have been better.' (1:56)

He refers to screenwriter and author David Trueba whose own contribution was rendered as part of Evarist Murtra's speech. Guardiola mentions a personal experience that fits perfectly. That is also an outstanding dialectic tool. By mentioning two famous individuals (Trueba and Laporta), he uses the well-known English technique known as name dropping (mentioning important names in passing). This allows him to generate interest and suspense.

'Because people say to me, "Good, good, you did well. You won what you won." All of these things. Yeah, yeah, we really can't complain...everything went well. But I know that I also have to impart knowledge to my players. There was a time when I had to learn it all, too. It wasn't like I borrowed it. All of the coaches that I had together gave it to me. All of them. Some naturally more than others, but every one of them made a contribution. That also includes all of my fellow players because I was a player and their teammate. But that also goes for the players whom I now have the pleasure of coaching. I've learned something from each one of them, and that isn't even something I should take pride in. That is how I live my job.' (2:37)

Pep's voice is firm. He isn't reading anything. He looks at the audience. He holds eye contact. He expresses an inner dialogue. It is an effective and attractive method of evoking people's fascination in a speech. At the same time, he reaffirms the importance of humility (or at least a certain claim to it) by recognising the contributions of others. Without saying so, he also praises the so-called 'intelligent organisation,' the ones who process, share and distribute recognition. He expresses this with a simple sentence: 'That is how I live my job.'

'I actually have only one thing to say; I love my job. I am full of passion for my profession. Believe me, I adore my job.' (2:45)

This is a crucial moment in his speech. There is no sign of nervousness. Now we experience the real Pep. He opens his heart to us and proclaims his message. He expresses exactly what Steve Jobs said in his memorable commencement address at Stanford University in the United States, 'Do what you love and love what you do.'

'I admired him when I was playing, and I admire him as a trainer. I also admire him when I talk about him. I admire him when I talk about this and that with others. Everything in our professional life and the positions we hold is ultimately reduced to just a few moments. Everything is summed up in one moment. In our job, there comes a time that fills us with deep satisfaction. We enjoy this time, and I would like to share this time with you.' (3:05)

He chooses a particular verb, 'admire,' and repeats it. This is a type of redundancy that promotes understanding of the message and makes one thing clear in the speech: Pep is a passionate person. It is the prelude to the climax of his speech. He speaks of magic moments and expresses the desire to share them with others (by which he shows his generosity and that he is in harmony with everyone listening to him; most likely the audience is already at his feet emotionally).

'I would like for people to know all of that. Before each game that we play, about one or two days before, I go into the basement of Can Barça where no outside light shines. There is a small office there that I have set up for myself. There is a rug in the office and a very good lamp. And I lock myself in this office.' (3:23)

It is a great moment in the speech. On one hand, he reveals something that awakens people's interest in him as a person (like a journalist or experienced public speaker who has a feeling for remarkable opportunities), and on the other, he expresses it in vivid language and with masterful intonation. The words 'small office' awaken a feeling of sobriety and strictness, while the detail of the rug communicates the impression that Pep tends to do things his way (which is also shown by the fact that he was responsible for the Barça team for five years).

'I lock myself in that office for one and a half to two hours. I take a few DVDs with me that Carles, Dome and Jordi have gathered for me. These are some of the people who help me like many others who are part of this adventure.' (3:36)

He again uses the technique of name-dropping mentioned previously in order to express public recognition for his closest staff members. The players of FC Barcelona are brilliant in handling the ball, but their coach does this with words.

'They give me a few DVDs about the team that we will be dealing with in a few days. I sit down, take a few sheets

of paper and a pen, put in the DVD and take a look at how our next opponent plays. I begin taking notes. "Wow! The right wing is strong! The right midfielder is stronger than the left. The right striker is faster than the left wing who likes to play long-balls. Another prefers a certain playing style. One prefers to climb the mountain on one side and go down on the other." And so I take note of everything that I can think of regarding the good qualities of the opposing team's players. In doing this, I also write down their weaknesses. "There, right there, we can really make them hurt! If I put one player here, Messi there and another in a staggered position, it could work."' (4:15)

Pep is in his element in this part of his speech. The use of various colloquial expressions lends him credibility and likability.

'Then comes the truly great, one might even say, fantastic, moment that holds the meaning of my profession. Believe me, that is exactly why I became a coach. For this moment. Everything else is fluff. Baggage that we carry along.' (4:29)

He arouses great expectations. The climax is coming closer. The tone in which he subsequently speaks of the President of the Generalitat is too suspiciously perfect to be spontaneous.

'I can very well imagine that the President of the Generalitat also has such moments as well as others, in which he has to stick to protocol. But it exists. That moment that

becomes precious when you notice it. Sometimes it lasts a minute and twenty seconds, sometimes a minute thirty, or a minute. Sometimes I have to watch two of the opponent's games. Eventually the moment comes when I say to myself, "Now we have them. We are going to win tomorrow."

I do not know why it is this way or whether you have seen certain things that give you this assurance. "We are going to win tomorrow."' (4:55)

He uses the succinct-sentence technique. This method is used to arouse interest, and it works just like a newspaper headline. Furthermore, he repeats himself. This is positive and reassuring redundancy. The idea is good and stands out.

'But please, don't think that I possess a...a magic formula. No, that is not how it is. I have always thought that before the game, but we have still lost several games. In this regard, this is obviously all just a theory. However, I am talking about it to explain my passion for my job.' (5:08)

He establishes a counterpoint of intentional humility. He makes his intentions clear: Don't think that I...

'I imagine that is exactly the same for you in your job. It must be the same everywhere in the world: doctors, bakers, physicians, school teachers bricklayers like my dad.' (5:17)

This is a moment of the greatest possible empathy in the speech. Empathy is the ability to put oneself in another's position. A good speaker must do this to establish an emotional bond and communicate his or her message effectively.

'Anyone could point out this moment in their profession. My moment confirms my love for my job. This moment is the reason I love it. When this moment comes, I have a responsibility and have to communicate the following to my team: "Lads, this is exactly what you have to do." Sometimes it works, sometimes not, but this moment, this very one, is the meaning of my job.' (5:35)

In a pleasant, albeit redundant, manner, he emphasises his most important message: he loves what he does.

'You will say, "Is that enough? Is that nice?" For me, it is. It is my destiny. This passion—I don't know where it comes from. The biggest thing that my father achieved was, I believe, buying a washing machine. I can't say anything about my grandfather on my father's side. I never met him as he passed away before I was born. As far as my mother goes, she had enough to do after the War. She had to go into hiding to avoid arrest. So there is actually nothing in my family history that can explain this gene. I don't know where it comes from, but that is how it is. I have this passion, and I feel it just as I did when I was little. People imparted this to me, this magic moment, this story that comes from within. This is what gives my job its meaning. Nothing else matters. And where does it all come from? As I said, I don't know, but it has really helped me.' (6:19)

Entirely consistent with the thoughts he has already introduced, Pep reinforces his message and enriches it with very personal details lending him much credibility. The allusion to his maternal grandfather and the War is entirely appropriate in light of the stage on which he is standing: the Parliament of Catalonia, a democratic institution that was suppressed during the Spanish Civil War.

'Here I would also like to talk about what a miracle sports are in and of themselves. Not football, but sports.' (6:25)

It is impressive how naturally he connects ideas. He uses short sentences when suitable and long ones when necessary. His intonation is masterful. In a written presentation, there would be a lot of italics. For example, he creates demand for a term that he just used for the first time himself: microclimate.

'My parents raised me, and they did this very well. Really very well. School helped me, of course. However, I was formed by the microclimate. The microclimate? Well, it is a sort of microsystem represented by a football team, a team that works together. That is where I learned to be the person I am today. I was formed by the fact that I played sports. That is where I learned what it means to win and to celebrate victories with the utmost humility.' (6:55)

This is one of the most impressive sentences when it comes to the expression of his values and also applies to the following statement on the role of a coach and the importance of being able to put oneself in another's position:

'I learned how to lose. It is really painful. It is defeat that teaches you to get back up again, and then you learn to value how difficult it is to win. I learned that a coach decides that I am not playing today because he has learned to think for everyone, while I was only thinking of myself. I learned that a teammate can be much better than I am and that he deserves to play. I learned that accusations and excuses are absolutely worthless. If you lose, you have only yourself to blame. If things do not go the way you want, it is your responsibility.' (7:21)

This is a declaration of principal reminiscent of the approach taken by writer and psychologist Antoni Bolinches in his books about the term personal maturity: 'We must not blame those around us for being the cause of our own poor qualities.'

'Sports had me from the time I was little with Barça. Barça embodied sports for me and was where I spent the most time playing them and gave everything to them. It made me the person I am today. I could go on about Barça, but I would like to digress a little so as to not speak about only it. Barça is my topic every three days at press conferences. Today I would only like to quote Valero Rivera, a wonderful handball coach who told me the following once when we were at the stadium:

"Barça makes us better people every day."

"Do you really think that?"

"Have no doubt! Live your job and thank this institution. And never ask anything in return. So never forget: Barça makes us all better people."' (8:09)

Mentioning Valero Rivera is not only another example of name-dropping and public recognition of others, but it is accompanied by another tool (which he repeats and uses effectively): short dialogue replay. This is a very journalistic and effective communication style used to render messages clearly and explicitly.

'And then there is one other thing that is ever present and that I make clear to my players and all those around us every day. We are very privileged!' (8:20)

Expressing gratitude is also a constant in Guardiola's oratory. It communicates humility, or at least counteracts envy in the face of such a large number of accomplishments in a cultural context, which anthropologically tends toward resentfulness.

'I am coming to the end. As Mònica very aptly said, at 23 I became a person of public interest, and at 40, the Gold Medal of this state's most important institution was hung around my neck. I find it much too early, but in part I am here because everything apparently went very well. We have won a lot recently, and naturally that has contributed to my being recognised. However, believe me when I say that I would be just as proud without all of those victories because the people that are out there, including me, have given everything so that things go well and they can be proud of us.' (9:00)

He uses the words 'coming to the end' to announce that he is about to conclude his remarks. This again attracts attention and serves to emphasise what follows. He reinforces this tool with the phrase, 'I would like to say one more thing.' If it is only one thing, the speech will truly soon be over...

'I would like to say one more thing. I do not want to be anyone's role model. I was born in a very small village not far from a larger town in the municipality of Bages. You know already that the village is called Santpedor. The nearest larger town is Manresa. As I said, I do not want to be a role model for anyone. I only want to follow my profession—a job that I love and that I want to do as

well as possible. I want for people to be able to discover this passion in what I do. Perhaps in a look, in my tone of voice, or in my gestures. I hope that people are able to see this passion and that it is transmitted further, that I am passing something on, that I can communicate what I feel. I am merely, at least I try to be, a good friend to my friends, people who I am sure to meet again after I have finally given up this compulsion to work. I have already lost many of them due to this pathological obsession. I am also only trying to be a good son to my parents and, first and foremost, a good partner to my life partner so that together we can enjoy the wonderful sight of seeing Maria, Màrius and Valentina grow up. We do not wish to interfere with their lives too much in doing so. They may fall as often as they like just as long as they know that their parents are there to pick them up again.' (10:13)

He again uses the opportunity to communicate humility. By expressing recognition for his village, Santpedor, he makes clear that he knows himself and that he is capable of a certain amount of self-criticism. However, in the end, he also emphasises his passion for what he does. An important message follows. He knows full well that there is life after football and reveals that he wants to be a good family man. He is a father who wants to give his children the opportunity to make mistakes without any stigmatisation.

'Mr President of Parliament, it a great honour for me and my family to receive this medal. We will try, I don't know when, to prove our gratitude to you. I only hope that

my behaviour will be as exemplary as possible...We must never forget that when we get up early, I mean really early, and we go to work without beating around the bush and making excuses, we are a state that no one can hold back. Believe me, we will be unstoppable then. Thank you and long live Catalonia!' (10:44)

The conclusion of a speech is the most important of all because it is the last impression that people keep in their minds. It may be that he was a little unsure in the beginning (the introduction of a speech is also important as it arouses interest and provides for a very particular atmosphere), but he ultimately also placed special emphasis on his spectacular closing. His conclusion contains a certain message, which he communicates in an understandable and succinct manner. So much so that his remark has already come to be fairly well known, even a little overused, misused and continuously paraphrased in our entertainment programmes. It is a brilliant phrase that also demonstrates a great deal of empathy. It shows that he has a feeling for the difficult history and social realities of an angry and disoriented society that needs to be motivated. The speech consists of 1,900 words spoken by a man of passion and offset with dialectic counterpoints. It acts like a true strength potion, a speech for a society out of balance.

THE 6:2 GENERATION

THE 6:2 GENERATION ■ ■ ■

I would like to make one thing plain. The term *6:2 Generation,* or *"Generación 2-6"* (in Spanish) is not merely a sociological label associated with the world of the Internet. This designation (created by me) refers to those who, in the prime of their life, experienced FC Barcelona's historic victory in Real Madrid's stadium on 2 May 2009.

The 6:2 victory was more than a feat of athletic of heroism. It was above all the culmination and result of an entire series of values ranging from self-sacrificing dedication, collective effort, clear principals and the beauty of the game to humility, generosity and enormous magnanimity.

That victory on May 2nd was more than just an episode. Just as the 5:0 triumph in 1974 proved the aspirations of the periphery by affirming that 'we are also here.' ('Capital 0, Periphery 5' was the title journalist Manuel Vázquez Montalbán, since deceased, gave to his article.) In the same way, the 6:2 result was proof of the intellect and cleverness of one of our own: Pep Guardiola.

This book is dedicated to his indisputable leadership qualities. May it survive the brief fire kindled by short-lived sporting successes in the media world.

I would like to show the value that made the extraordinary transformation of the blue-red team possible. It is a team that had its fans and all of the club's stakeholders almost doubting in their ability three years prior but then sent the whole world into raptures. Today, the city of Barcelona and Catalan society is in the centre of global public attention and simultaneously provides a new paradigm in football. It is a philosophy of this sport based on the Guardiola method, that is to say, 'Made in Catalonia'.

> *Football is in a position to establish its brand in the eyes of the global public. Barça is currently one of the most prestigious brands on our planet. Pep Guardiola is in turn the undisputed top brand in Catalonia.*

A DAY TO REMEMBER AT ESADE

On 17 April 2009, I had the privilege of attending the presentation ceremony of former FC Barcelona vice president Ferran Soriano's book titled *La pelota no entra por azar* (The Ball Doesn't Go In By Chance) at the ESADE Business School in Barcelona.

There was no longer any doubt. This presentation definitively established cultural legitimacy of the body of literature dedicated to the topic of leadership and sports.

It was a long process, but it is no longer considered sacrilege that the academic world is also occupying itself with what happens on the pitch. The world of academies and universities is opening up during these times of crisis and brutal competition we are experiencing today and feels no shame whatsoever in doing so.

Of course, the media glamour of football also has something to do with this phenomenon. Football is a topic that moves the masses, and, at the same time, it is an area in which proven specialists are in demand. The media serve as a sounding board in this regard.

The goal is to be noticed. A plethora of books have come out recently that draw a connection between football and leadership. In actuality, there is a large market for such works. The desire to experience more is enormous. As a lecturer at various economics universities, I can only attest to this. Some time ago, I began gathering and analysing documents on Pep Guardiola's development as a manager and his way of dealing with the human resources he manages.

However, my interest is nothing new and did not just develop recently.

I recall my first article on football and management in the early 1990s. I was still studying, at least part-time, for my MBA at ESADE and simultaneously working for *Avui* magazine (initially as editor-in-chief and later as deputy director on weekends).

Thanks to the support of journalist Martí Anglada, I was allowed to write a weekly page on management. It was a collection of news and reviews on the topic that I selected from a veritable mountain of expert articles (mostly in English).

I remember that one of these articles was titled 'Management sobre el césped' ('Management on the Turf'). I dedicated it to the effective (and also contested) leadership of Johan Cruyff, the Barça coach at the time. He would not hesitate to criticise a player to the press in order to make him angry and thus motivate him to give it his best in the next game.

Many of my articles must have been seen as somewhat eccentric at that time. Some of the people who most likely read me in secret were also probably present at Soriano's ESADE book presentation and were among those applauding with delight. That is how it is. Both times and customs change.

I remember how I once wrote about how Cruyff used the Pygmalion effect with goalkeeper Busquets (father of current midfielder Sergio Busquets). It is an effective means of improving others by creating heightened expectations (instead of seeing to believe, the idea is to believe in order to see).

This article was met surprisingly with humorous commentaries from Antoni Bassas and Xavi Bosch on *Alguna pregunta més?* (Any more questions?), a midnight programme on Catalunya Ràdio that entertains people with notes on the day's events, games, jokes and displays of disrespect. The commentaries on my article were deliberately cheeky remarks broadcasted on public radio.

However, football, like essentially everything in life, possesses a certain management component. For this reason, I am pleased that the business schools of the sports world are opening up even if it is only to avoid losing students in these times of bitter struggle for positions in international quality rankings. There is nothing that the leadership at these educational institutions fear more. (In this regard, these institutions are more a force for evil than good.)

Today, I still remember with pleasure that article that I wrote for *Avui* titled *"No dejes que una escuela de negocios te arruine la vida"* [Don't Let a Business School Ruin Your Life]. I was inspired to write it by the photocopy distribution department at ESADE. The photocopies were never delivered on time and paradoxically this was especially true when we had a course on management logistics. It was neither logical nor logistical. However, the lesson to be learned was obvious. A business school is itself not obligated to apply the rules it is meant to communicate.

> *It is difficult to preach a sustainable leadership style if you yourself do not lead the way with concrete actions and by setting a good example.*

CAN YOU BELIEVE IN MIRACLES?

I would like to admit outright that I am both intrinsically and extrinsically a big sceptic. If journalism, a profession about which I have no illusions, is capable of communicating one thing, it is realism. The world is the way it is. And if it should no longer be there, it will simply no longer exist.

However, I must also concede the two years from the end of 2008 until 2010 seemed to me to be a true miracle for FC Barcelona. A squad more or less at the same level as the previous year was completely transformed by Pep Guardiola in order to optimise the available human resources in a superb manner. It was a feat worthy of being described in a book in excruciating detail. It was a fantastic performance that teaches us lessons for the future. There is no doubt that

> *success has something to do with a team's total performance, like the 'e' in 'team.'*

It was a combination of the talents of many that made the successes of these two unforgettable years possible. This required a conductor, and Pep was the great Maestro of this orchestra. It is for all of these accomplishments that he is rendered public recognition. However, his accomplishments are not only athletic in nature. He triumphed as a manager. This means brilliance in the fields of human resource leadership and organisation, personnel leadership, talent optimisation and overcoming cultural differences.

Working in a team is no walk in the park. Doing this with such a heterogeneous and international squad as FC Barcelona requires tremendous abilities in dealing with cultural differences, the strong Catalan component notwithstanding.

How often have projects failed due to an inability to weld together a team of players with highly varied backgrounds? The ability to successfully lead culturally diverse groups is extremely important in this interconnected, interdependent, globalised world.

Pep Guardiola has proven himself a forward-thinking man of the world in this area. He already has personal experience with other countries and cultures (Italy, United Arab Emirates, Mexico). He speaks several languages (Catalan, Spanish, English, Italian). He is a fan of music from other countries. He loves trying exotic new tastes and flavours. He is an avid reader. He likes poetry, and sometimes he even writes.

He is a citizen of the world but a Catalan to his core. His unmatched blend of talent and dedication made it possible to reap these fruits that so delight the sporting palate.

The magic formula: Talent + Dedication

It is actually quite simple.

The pre-Guardiola squad by no means lacked talent. What it was missing was dedication in the sense of self-sacrifice. This was because of Frank Rijkaard's (the coach at that time) lack of leadership qualities.

This lack of dedication essentially arose from a lack of hunger for success on the pitch and no desire to win, to triumph and to be challenged.

It is not just a matter of working with talented players, who must also be willing to give their all. Though this is practically unachievable without a leader who propels them and demands dedication.

Pep Guardiola managed to arouse self-sacrifice in his players, as he is himself a perfect role model of dedication. This sort of self-sacrifice is part of his very core.

Dedication also involves participation. Participation produces motivation. One wants to do what one has to do. It is just a question of getting to work.

Good leaders discover talents and awake in them self-sacrifice and the hunger for success without being affected by cultural differences. They know how to interpret such differences and how to deal with them. These are leaders who lead by example and thereby demonstrate their dedication.

ON THE COACH WHO ALSO MAKES ISOLATED DECISIONS

The evening before the historic 6:2 victory in Bernabéu Stadium (2 May 2009), Climent, a good friend from Torelló and frequent guest in Vidrà (near Bisaura between Osona and Ripollès, my paradise in the Pyrenean foothills) told me that Guardiola often puts substitute players in the game in order to placate them. For my friend, this signified a lack of authority.

'The best should always play, and that's that!' he explained.

I held, in contrast, that the players on the substitute bench play an important role over the course of a long and hard season. They would be neither motivated nor really available if they were not able to prove themselves.

That is exactly what Pep Guardiola did, and he repeatedly said in public that he is sad that he cannot let everyone play, as all of them were so incredibly talented.

I believe that the young FC Barcelona coach also proves to be a great sports psychologist in this instance. He was once a player himself and knows very well how important it is that a coach be able to depend on someone.

The fact that Busquets and Bojan were also on the pitch in the last minutes of that remarkable game on 2 May 2009 is evidence that he also wanted to allow those who were not in the starting line-up to have a part in the fun and the team's success.

It is fundamentally important to maintain the moral of a squad. For this reason, one must use small gestures to demonstrate that one also depends on these players. There must be no doubt of this whatsoever.

The *holy cows*, meaning the big stars, have earned their own capital. How do you milk them? How do you coddle them without spoiling them too much?

There is no doubt in the squad's football abilities, but the degree of their commitment and dedication must initially be adjusted by hand. That was the exact deciding factor that initially made the Guardiola miracle possible.

> *The conclusiveness of a leader's actions is not based on his or her ability to keep everyone satisfied or by doing what the majority expects. It is expressed in how one reconciles one's thoughts with one's actions and one's action's with one's thoughts. This is often done in the face of popular opinion and by making isolated decisions.*

MAKING OTHERS HAPPY

'I know that we made many people happy today. I am truly happy about this.' Those were Pep Guardiola's words at the press conference after the historic 6:2 win in Bernabéu Stadium.

What beautiful words! He should have also added, 'and that is what gives my life purpose.'

Because that is the reality.

The leader Pep Guardiola's enormous generosity stands out most of all, a generosity which can reach the point of self-abandonment in all of his endeavours. His advancing baldness and his exhausted facial expression appear to be the consequences of the excessive passion that he lives and dedicates to the game of football.

One could justifiably refer here to the masterful statement by Apple founder Steve Jobs in his legendary commencement speech at Stanford University, which can also be found online: 'Do what you love and love what you do.'

The devotion that Guardiola feels for football is exemplary. He gives body and soul to the game. All of his talent, which is abundant, is combined with the greatest possible dedication. Pep embodies the magic T + D formula:

> *Talent + Dedication.*
> *Both factors are equally required.*

Choose your human resources carefully and offer them an environment in which they can constantly develop as people. If you make them big, they will make you big in turn. You will grow together.

A leader must lead by setting a good example in order to live up to these high expectations. He must be the first one to demonstrate all of his abilities and have new possible solutions prepared at all times. He has to pay attention to the small details that make the decisive difference.

> *If you want to have a team of unbeatable players, lead them as though they are such. The leader is the mirror that reflects everyone else. Great leaders ensure that their people are also great. No one will follow leaders who lack greatness.*

THE POWER TO CHANGE

There are many different types of leaders. Once, when I was discussing this topic with ESADA director general, Carlos Losada Marrodán, he made the following remarkable comment:

'There are hundreds of books about leading people.'

He had dealt with this topic in depth during his research in the United States at the Kennedy School in Harvard (political science and management), which I have visited often of late. With every visit, I could also see that more and more new books have been written on the topic.

But what is a leader? Or to be more precise, what distinguishes a leader who is capable of changing people?

Maybe they have to be like Pep Guardiola, someone who has what it takes to alter the preferences and attitudes of his protégés and get the best out of them. That means being a *positive booster,* a person who draws the right lessons out of circumstances and becomes stronger and more mature.

On 5 May 2009, the Tuesday three days after the 6:2 game in Bernabéu Stadium, Guardiola surprised the world by putting his players' euphoria in check in a composed and earnest tone. They were now meant to think about the semi-final the next day against Chelsea. They had not yet won the final in Rome. First they had to clear the Chelsea hurdle.

This ability to calibrate his players mentally is the Barça coach's great achievement. It requires respect, clear perception and the ability to implement these things and continue down the given path. This means he has to be credible. Guardiola has made students and flowerers of the truth out of his players. He is, pardon the expression, a preacher. He proclaimed his message, and it was received.

Is he a sort of football Messiah? In any case, he is a charismatic leader. That means he is attractive and likable. He invites people to follow and believe in him. We are happy when he smiles. He ensures that he is loved.

He is a leader who is capable of changing others so that they give their best. That is the most impressive task of all great leaders. It is the task that results in the most accomplishments and comes the closest to a being a small miracle when it is achieved.

We already know the fruits reaped from talent and dedication.

Leaders with values leave a trail behind and pull their people along with them.

They change their protégés. They enable them to find the best in themselves. They create dedication.

This is why they are loved. They are simply attractive people.

SHARED ALIGNMENT

I would like to use an English term to emphasise the importance of this approach: alignment. In other words, it means queuing up behind the one directing and following that person right down the marked path—everyone in step, everyone in the same direction.

This is also something that is visible in a team's external communications. It is plain to see that the players who express themselves publically repeat the same message. The message is received and then internalised. There are no deviations whatsoever. Every member of the team speaks with one voice, and thus various sources proclaim the same message. The great power of persuasion is demonstrated, and the group manifests unity.

The author of these lines has been training people in public speaking for many years and knows a lot about promoting a common alignment within the walls of an organisation. It is one of the most difficult and important tasks and reveals the level of discipline in the organisation. It is also indicative of whether one believes in the power of communication and perceives it as a strategic tool.

Of course, the whole world cannot dance to the beat of this drum.

In addition, explanations should be conclusive and shared by all who speak publically on behalf of the team, in other words, the team's spokespersons.

There are always discrepancies among spokespersons, but Pep Guardiola solved this problem. He practices a headline culture. He knows that the press is constantly in need of new and resounding headlines. His spokespersons provide exactly that by propagating their headlines with apparent spontaneity. That is the quintessence of a good spokesperson: being believable and meeting journalists halfway.

It is the oil in the engine. It is the petrol that ensures the vehicle remains in motion.

Pep Guardiola would be an outstanding communications director in a multinational corporation (and surely many other things as well).

In actuality, that's what Barça is already: a major multinational media corporation that sees itself as a global brand.

> *Everyone always tugs on the same rope.*
> *That is shared alignment. Everyone is in*
> *the right lane and has internalised this.*
> *For those who act as spokespersons, the*
> *message is always conclusive and never*
> *improvised. This coherence is what*
> *makes the message convincing.*

PLAYER 'VIBRATIONS'

'I feel when we are going to win in the vibrations of my players.'

That is the content of the text message that several journalists closest to Guardiola received just hours before the Real Madrid–Barcelona match on 2 May 2009.

It is Pep's general practice to share his impressions with a group of trusted journalists. His network is comprehensive and fully devoted to him. This allows him to network efficiently, which is indispensable in an environment as turbulent as Barça. The term *vibrations* speaks to his way of intuitively predicting the course of events. He could just as well have said that he can smell it when his team is going to win, or that he feels it, or that he senses it through some other extremity. However, Pep favours the term *vibrations*. I do not know if this is an expression typical of his favourite

poet Miquel Martí i Pol, but it is exactly in tune with the very best representatives of the Generation of '27 (Federico García Lorca, Luis Cernuda and other poets).

The truth is that the blue-red side delivered a great performance at Bernabéu. They wanted everyone to see it after the many unkind comments regarding the season's progress up to that point, comments that also tended to exude a certain distain for their previous successes. By the way, this was also to be repeated in the following season when a portion of the press in Madrid coined the term *Villarato*, alluding to the alleged bias for the Catalan team among the referees in La Liga.

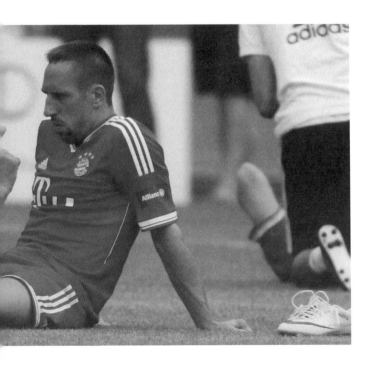

On 2 May 2009, the squad offered one of the best performances in FC Barcelona history. That is exactly what Pep had hoped for, or instinctively anticipated.

The origin of this instinct lies in the fact that he knows his players very well and is always very close to them. Let's not deceive ourselves. We are not talking about the magic potion of Asterix and Obelix or the paranormal powers of a reborn professor Fassman, that mysterious sorcerer from the region of Pallars (famous hypnotist and magician of the 1950s and 1960s). We are simply talking about knowing the people one works with in order to get a feeling for the group's state of mind. This means knowing the team's mood, something one fosters in order to win.

It was very simple. The entire team furiously desired to express one thing, *'Enough!'*

APPRECIATION FOR LIFE

Pep Guardiola displays his appreciation constantly. He is well aware of his privileged status. To a certain extent, we were (and are) all privileged through the gift of life. We are alive and that is a wonderful thing in itself (the extent to which we are aware of this is another issue).

Pep Guardiola knows very well that he lives in extraordinary circumstances. A mere two years after being chosen as the coach of FC Barcelona, he had won no less than seven of the nine possible titles: 2 La Liga championships, 1

Copa del Rey, 1 Champions League Cup, 1 Supercopa de España, 1 UEFA Super Cup and 1 FIFA Club World Cup.

That is impressive. No Spanish team before had managed such a feat. The La Liga–Copa del Rey–Champions League triple had never before been achieved.

This appreciation for life is surely the source of many wonderful things that have happened around him. Pep directly exudes the aura of a 'person who was chosen to win.' He is a sort of 'Invictus,' a born winner, a Nelson Mandela of football. He is a leader who accomplishes more than the others above all because he has done one thing his entire life: He has observed. He is a walking sponge that constantly soaks up new knowledge and understanding.

Pep Guardiola has made this element of appreciation the fulcrum of his methodology and operational principle.

At the same time, he knew how to surround himself with protégés. The Guardiola's doctrine is very effective because he is more than a coach. He is a person who understands how to love.

DOES PEP HAVE ANY

WEAKNESSES AT ALL?

DOES PEP HAVE ANY WEAKNESSES AT ALL? ■ ■ ■

THE INIESTA PHENOMENON

Andrés Iniesta's divine goal against FC Chelsea (06 May 2009) made headlines across all the media, both general and sports news. It was the apex of an almost meteoric development.

Iniesta has since been recognised as one of the five best footballers in the world despite the fact that he was continuously out of the game during the following season due to injuries.

> *'The god of football has arrived at*
> *Stamford Bridge.*
> *The god of football justice.'*
> *(Canal Plus TV after Iniesta's goal)*

In never ceases to amaze when an athlete possesses an abundance of three things: magic feet, a bright mind and a humble heart.

One could also describe his humility with the term rooted. He kept both feet firmly planted on the ground, on the earth—the origin of life. He is a realist.

Such humility is the best antidote to arrogance as well as to decline. It is an exemplary type of humility that surpasses the colours of a particular football club and is met time and again with the applause of not only one's own fans but also of the fans of the opposing team (with the possible exception of the unfortunate Chelsea fans).

One of the most wonderful spectacles of 2009 and 2010 was to see how two of the Barcelona players, Iniesta and Xavi, received the applause of all of the Spanish fans when entering and leaving the pitch. It was an impressive, contagious and profound sort of recognition, a true inspiration.

Football has always been a blend of passion and misery in which defeating the opponent is often held above accentuating one's own strengths. It is a sort of war marketing in which destruction is more important than building.

Guardiola's Barça won in elegant fashion and put its sportsmanlike competitive spirit front and centre as the essence of its values.

In these times of values crisis, an entire football teams subscribes to one goal: to win with decency.

It doesn't get any better than that.

Players like Iniesta ('Don Andrés' as he was so aptly called by radio host Joaquim Maria Puyal) are symbols of this moral revolution. They break with the recent past and focus on the future.

And now we have before us an immaculate Barça squad that places the essence of football over pure sporting rivalry.

> *We are witnessing a two-sided spectacle: great football and sporting decency. The applause of the opponent is the highest recognition. It is the purest of all victories.*

WHEN THE CAMERAS ARE RUNNING

I would like to apologise for this, but I feel compelled to somewhat demystify the image of professional footballers. In actuality, many of them are mere swindlers and actors when it comes to expressing themselves publically or celebrating a goal on the pitch.

Their collective intellectual behaviour reflects our expectations of them even if there are certain exceptions. However, as soon as they discover the breast of the media (whose milk is indubitably sweet), they suckle with boundless fervour. They invent gestures, develop signature ways of celebrating goals and reveal astonishing messages written under their jerseys, and all of this is the result of plans and strategies that are anything but spontaneous.

It comes out during press conferences time and again. Many football pros have never read a book with the possible exception of their family records, and even that must have been rather difficult for them. Even in this regard, Pep Guardiola is an extraordinary counterexample. In a career field full of hardnosed ignoramuses, he can appreciate culture. He is a rare bird in this respect.

This fact was also parodied in the *Crackòvia* comedy programme in which the players discover a lone book in Oleguer's old locker, and Valdés asks coach Guardiola 'how to turn it on' (not because he thinks it's an eBook).

Some players conceal their lack of culture by strictly holding to the advice of specialists in their environment. The well-loved behaviour of constantly repeating clichés should be mentioned here as it is more than abundant in football.

In any case, the players know the stadium cameras record sound and like to take advantage of this. As a result, there is what plays out in front of the cameras, and there is the reality behind closed doors.

'If people were to see how the players are behind closed doors, they would be very surprised,' admitted a high-level functionary of the Catalan team once who was on very

good terms with the players. They are not better or worse. They are simply different.

The importance of the media in football stipulates the public behaviour if its protagonists. We get a distorted picture of many players. Culture and education are not exactly their strength.

AN EXCEPTIONAL EMBRACE

Toward the end of the Chelsea-Barcelona game in Guardiola's first season in the Champions League, he embraced the opposing coach, Guus Hiddink, as if to congratulate him with his forthcoming victory. Just a few seconds later, Iniesta made his goal and everything changed.

However, this embrace and the smile he displayed in doing so were exceptional. It was impressive. It revealed the elegance of a loser who subsequently did not lose.

Television made these images immortal just as it has done with many others of the telegenic FC Barcelona coach. These are images that have already become part of our television culture.

This embrace had a very special meaning. It was a young man's acknowledgement of his elder. It expressed something positive. It was an embrace that stated, 'Well

I did what I could!' It was an embrace given as a noble gesture by the loser who was also simultaneously a moral winner.

Jordi Juste, the youth academy coach and journalist (former Tokyo correspondent of *El Periódico* newspaper) who arrived in Catalonia from Japan in 2009, told me, 'Guardiola loves life and is thankful for all of the wonderful things it has given him. Life thanks him in return with ever-increasing privileges.'

Jordi put it very well with almost far-eastern wisdom. That is why I quoted him here.

There is a reason that one of Guardiola's favourite songs is *Viva la Vida* by Coldplay. The song exudes an incredible amount of enthusiasm and *joie de vivre* even if the media did somewhat spoil the effect for us by playing it constantly as the anthem of both of the ever-successful seasons.

Here we see Guardiola's taste in music and his ability to use music in a targeted manner. In this specific instance, he used it as an unremitting means of encouraging and motivating his players game after game.

> *A sense of appreciation for life. A grateful leader demonstrates positive behaviour and shares it with others. Thankfulness also means generosity. The more we give, the more we receive.*

DOES THIS BLOKE HAVE ZERO WEAK POINTS?

I have asked the following question of those associated with the trainer numerous times: What are Pep Guardiola's weaknesses?

A former director of the club gave a representative answer:

'He is stubborn.'

This term should be analysed in context. Here, stubborn means that when he does not like something, he does not suppress it but rather removes and banishes it from his thoughts. In other words, it's over! A new game will bring new luck!

I also asked this same functionary, 'Can he take a lot [if things do not go well someday]?'

'Time will tell. If one disregards the first two games of his first season that began with an away defeat and a draw at home, Guardiola had a very good season, and his second season was brilliant as well.'

As he was so successful so soon after starting, we cannot say to what point he would have withstood an unsympathetic mass media over a longer period of time. Such an instance has not yet occurred in his career.

All of that is surely true. Then again, the fact that he moved to La Masía youth academy when he was just 13 and asserted himself there as a very young player shows that that there exists an iron-willed, indomitable Pep. This was also demonstrated in his long legal battle in Italy over doping accusations against him.

One could also accuse him of having the means at hand that no other coach had ever had at his disposal.

That is surely true. The coaching staff at Pep's disposal is comprised of more than 30 people who are proven specialists in their fields. They have access to an incredible range of resources and perform first-class work. As a whole, they are a not–so-insignificant budget item for the club.

However, it should also be kept in mind that he chose these people and connected them with the club. He included this as a mandatory condition for his project. He knew how to protect his project and convince FC Barcelona of the need to put everything he wanted in his control. This also goes for the two expensive and contested transfers that did not exactly bring what had been hoped for. I am talking about Zlatan Ibrahimovic and Dmytro Tschyhrynskyj.

Towards the end of his second season, both signings proved to be mistakes and provided for the most controversy in Guardiola's track record as coach of Barcelona.

The Ibrahimovic case was hotly disputed. A lot of money was put on the table for him. At the same time, the team lost Eto'o when he transferred to Inter, the team that kept Barcelona from reaching the Champions League final and ultimately won the title in May of 2010 in Santiago Bernabéu Stadium where the Catalan team would have so gladly played.

Tschyhrynskyj's signing was subjected to intense criticism due to the high price paid for the young Ukrainian. He played defence and had not yet matured as a player. In addition to that, the club had initially been against the transfer. In the end, Tschyhrynskyj hardly played at all

The 2009 Tschyhrynskyi transfer: a fleck on Guardiola's white vest.

during the season, and he did anything but impress the Barça fans in the few games he did play.

Is Guardiola stubborn in the face of all reason? Is he a money-waster? Is he too spoiled?

Guardiola's reputation was tarnished by both decisions in terms of his demands to sign new players. However, the exact opposite happened with the development of Sergio Busquets, Pedrito, Thiago, Fontàs, Cuenca, Tello, Montoya, Sergi Roberto, Muniesa and Bartra, players from FC Barcelona's own youth academy. Contesting a major final with 11 home-grown players is a dream that can very well come true.

In regards to his public demeanour, it is true that although Guardiola has established himself as a well-respected pro in his field, he definitely shows signs of his stress on the coaches' bench, distributes elbow blows and emits angry comments about referees, a tendency which has many times resulted in him being exiled to the stands.

Those that know him well note that he displays manic behaviour and exhibits an almost pathological desire for perfection at times. However, all of that is for a good cause, namely to achieve excellence.

A sports journalist who has followed Pep's career from the very beginning also notes:

'Pep will never admit that a game cannot be won because there is no reason to do so. He always wants to find a reason for everything.'

In this respect, he has an almost scientific point of view on football. When he fails to win a game, he analyses it time and again until he finds an explanation.

Then again, this compulsion to have control over every detail and devote himself to every trifle can lead to fatigue and have negative effects on his health. That was already demonstrated by Johan Cruyff many times.

Fortunately, when it comes to his family life, Pep has excellent support. His wife Cristina takes care of the house and their three children. Cristina takes on the responsibility for the household and is extremely discrete, always remaining in Pep's shadow. Those who know her praise her character and highlight her good influence.

Cristina studied information science at university and met Pep at her parents' boutique in Manresa where she worked.

Could it be said regarding the circumstances of Guardiola's switch to the Barça coach's bench that he took advantage of a historic opportunity? The situation was as follows: The president, Joan Laporta, was about to lose his office; Guardiola had attained great reputation as a former player of the club; and they needed to find a miracle cure for a president who was on the ropes...

A high-ranking club functionary reported to me about what happened:

'When we informed him that we had selected him to coach Barça, he said, "You did the right thing. Now we will win the championship!"'

Overconfident? Even arrogant?

Actually not, and facts are definitely on his side.

A visionary? A know-it-all? A messiah?

Well, the only thing that we know is that he has always worked hard and that he has gained everything he has by the sweat of his brow.

This can be proven. The rest is simply conjecture.

'If he has a weakness, it his deep lack of trust.'

Then again, he knows exactly whom he can trust. He is also a good listener, as I was assured by a former board member of the club who knows every facet of the Barça coach's career, including very private details. Football is a very special industry, in which distrust is more than justified according to the former board member who is also a historic personality in the club. Others confirm that Guardiola is a 'football madman.' I assume that the madness is more of a burden and something negative because it can be unsettling. However, if we replace the term madness with extreme passion, we have a more positive attribute.

At the same time, Guardiola reveals himself to be a highly sensitive person, very emotional and easy to upset in the company of smaller groups. A close colleague of the Catalan coach once revealed that Pep had told him during a mobile phone conversation that he would resign because a player's behaviour had disappointed him so deeply. He backpedalled the next day. Apparently it was not as bad as all that in the end.

Television cameras show how Guardiola gesticulates on the bench. At the Sevilla-Barcelona game last season, both gesticulation and elbow blows were to be seen when the Catalan team was leading 3:0 and allowed two balls into their own net within a few minutes. Guardiola's reacted with scarcely containable fury.

In any case, Guardiola always communicates pure passion and a high level of energy on the bench.

Pep Guardiola's communication skills make him very persuasive, especially with the female population. Surveys have confirmed time and again that he is the most favoured coach among women. No one is as sexy and erotic as he is. Many women have all of a sudden become interested in football since he entered the public eye. Things that used to bore them to tears they now find interesting.

However, this ability to communicate can also have a negative effect. This becomes especially evident when he announces subtle messages, addresses very specific groups of fans or when his abundant politeness is construed as insincerity and he is accused of attempting to curry favour or avoid saying what he really thinks. I shall never forget the press conference at the 2010 Expo-Management forum in Madrid when I presented 'The Guardiola Method.' When the time came to ask questions of the author, a woman from Madrid stepped forward and asked me, with emotion in her voice and a blissful look on her face:

'Is Pep really like you describe him?'

As I travel throughout Spain explaining the Guardiola method, I encounter people time and again who have contrived their own version of people, their own personal José Hucha. They want to admire one of their own in whom they can see a reflection of themselves. In this regard, admiration is the prevailing feeling. When it comes to football on the Iberian Peninsula, the Spanish national team coach, Vincente del Bosque, a polite man, is probably the one who is most similar to Pep Guardiola in terms of common sense.

Of course, not everything about Pep is pleasant. Football is passion and heartfelt emotion. The achievements of others remind many of their own weaknesses. The audience includes all sorts of people, and such a long winning streak naturally evokes envy, every sort of suspicion imaginable and the hidden desire for there to actually be something dirty or furtive going on even if it is only false humility, double standards or the desire to exploit others.

Some media representatives in the sports world feel it is their calling to find a person's weak points and to jump on every suspicious indication thereof. There is a major market for this.

Pep's personality is a combination of introversion and strong character. He tends towards clear ideas, prefers to do things his way and is simultaneously tough with people in his environment who disappoint him.

He is a person who sees himself as an object of desire and will not become trapped by those who are trying to exploit him. In this regard, he understands the most subtle exploitation techniques, and some have no doubt that he uses them. In any case, such techniques are not unfamiliar to him.

There is one thing that is very impressive about Guardiola's press conferences (there have already been more than 500): the unbelievable speed with which he identifies who is asking him a question and how his face betrays what he thinks about that person. This reaction shows us not only how quickly he thinks but also how swiftly he forms his opinion. This reveals his incredibly expressive personality. The paradox is that there is also a phlegmatic and at times even extremely diplomatic Pep interspersed with a Pep whose blood seems to be boiling.

Does this constantly impolite, unruly and disappointing Pep exist? I hear all sorts of stories time and again, but many of them are very difficult to verify. When a person is exposed to such frequent and extensive public scrutiny, his or her weak moments and inappropriate reactions are likely to be special attention. Of course, such a massive amount of social success can result in a person letting down their guard and revealing the exhaustion behind the success.

You should watch Pep sometime at the beginning of a press conference as he sits there in a storm of camera flashes. He just allows this gratification-seeking ceremony to be carried out over him.

> *Great leaders and geniuses share a passion for what they do. Of course, this passion can also become an obsession, as they are far more dedicated to their cause compared to other mortals.*

THE CLUB &

ITS BLUE-RED SOUL

THE CLUB &
ITS BLUE-RED SOUL ■ ■ ■

One of the most common explanations for Guardiola's success is that he knows the club inside and out.

Guardiola began living in Barcelona very early, initially at La Masía where he was also a ball boy, then as a player, former player, Barcelona B-squad coach and so on.

His success shows us how important it is to know an organisation if one desires to serve it effectively. One has to get to its very core, know its soul, its genetic code, its anthropological conditioning, the unseen series of assistants and its cultural features. One has to know practically everything that leaves a trace. History is not just starting with us (a misperception called *adamism*). There are always earlier people and events that one has to know.

However, more than anything, one has to understand the meaning of the following key phrase: Barça is more than a club. It would be difficult to coach the first squad without being aware of the full scope of what is known as *barcelonism*.

The Dutchman Louis van Gaal was a historic example of ignorance in this respect. He was probably the most sincere coach in the club's history but was paradoxically also despised by the press. He was criticised primarily for his temperament, his manners...and his ignorance. This was not associated with his playing tactics but rather his emotional ones and because he did not know the institution and did not understand its blue-red soul.

An example of this emotional myopia was the insensitive way in which he got rid of former player Guillermo Amor, a symbol of the La Masía youth academy's outstanding work.

Guardiola is exactly the opposite. He demonstrates a meticulous and detail-enamoured sort of knowledge and a level of awareness almost reminiscent of feminine intuition in the best possible sense. He has an analytical character and above all a calling. To paraphrase, he does what he loves and he loves what he does.

Guardiola was born for the game of football. He dedicates himself to this sport neck and crop and uses his love of detail as a deadly weapon. He possesses a powerful intellect, grasps the minutest details with astonishing celerity and knows how to put himself in the position of others. These important virtues may also be described as empathy. And Van Gaal, well he didn't possess a single one of them.

There they are again—those cultural differences that one simply has to know.

> *A good leader knows the terrain around him perfectly. He immerses himself in the DNA of his organisation.*

One must have a sense for cultural specifics and know how to deal with them.

Barça, as an institution, has its own soul, which is rooted in its history. When going to a new place, one must be aware of its history.

Because history does not begin with our arrival.

TALKING FOR THE SAKE OF TALKING

There was a time in Catalonia when discussions on the possibility of Pep Guardiola being homosexual were almost as frequent as conversations about football.

The assertions of alleged homosexuality at that time were yet another attempt to degrade the person in question. At best, this demonstrated a certain lack of consideration intertwined with an accusation. Have you heard that Guardiola…and so on and so forth.

A friend of Pep's family told me that these rumours started when he picked up his fiancée Cristina (now his wife and mother of his three children) in a neighbourhood of the Gracia district containing numerous bars frequented by homosexuals at that time.

The rumours spread further when AIDS came into the picture. Some saw his lean ascetic facial features as the first symptoms of the disease.

'He really has become very thin,' could often be heard and was said in a way that implied a very particular something.

Next, accusations of doping in Italy provided for a new wave of unfriendly comments. Pep did not let on that he noticed any of it. It isn't easy when you are under suspicion and the media descends on you with furious determination to make a profit out of the whole affair. The more extreme the news, the better it is for them.

Pep always watches what they are doing. Everything is up for grabs for the newspapers and mass media in general.

They have to sell, sell, sell. That is their compulsion. They have to talk for the sake of talking, even if it means bringing someone down in doing so. I admit, they also provide information from time to time.

But Pep did not stumble.

In the end, he managed to convince everyone of his innocence. It was ultimately his stubbornness that enabled him to restore this honour in the world of sports.

> *The media makes or breaks a modern leader. The ability to withstand media pressure is a must-have in the repertoire of anyone leading an organisation open to public scrutiny such as a first-class football club.*

A CATALAN OBAMA?

At times Pep Guardiola is spoken of as if he were a Catalan Obama. This is not without reason. Both are modern, relatively young, elegant, athletic and great communicators as well as persuaders. In any case, they evoke trust. They appear credible and also communicate the impression that they believe in the people. They both came along in times of crisis and are viewed as trustworthy. That is the most valued characteristic, and it is also very difficult to achieve. How often has that very thing resulted in failure?

Press conferences provide an example of his temperance and professionalism. He requests that all who want to ask him a question state their name and the organisation they represent. He responds to questions in the language in which they are asked if he can. No topic is off limits, and he even becomes energetic if he believes that a journalist's question holds value. His arguments are precise and logical. He demonstrates that he is extremely well informed and read concerning all topics of current interest.

In addition, Guardiola has proven to be resourceful when it comes to communicating news that lighten the burden of journalists who are always on the lookout for headlines.

In contrast, he gives no interviews. This displeases the media, but his own people understand it. Guardiola simply could not keep everyone satisfied, and it would eventually cause undesirable unequal treatment.

We are dealing with a leader in the field of sports who is extremely skilled in dealing with the media and speaks in hair-splitting detail at press conferences. Even the journalists must admit that the quality of Barça press conferences has improved considerably since the lad from Santpedor has been around.

In contrast, Joan Laporta is a good example of how quickly one can lose prestige and take many missteps. His election victory was impressive. He won the voters over with his confident demeanour and dynamism. He was telegenic, had the members practically in the palm of his hand and gained the confidence of everyone.

However, unexpectedly for everyone, he quickly lost the credit he had gained due to his absurd and seemingly arrogant behaviour. He provoked incidents resulting in negative headlines, although fortunately no pictures were taken. In one instance, he pulled down his pants at the metal detector in Prat airport because he was annoyed by the security measures in place. Another time, he was seen hurling insults at his driver in public.

The president previously considered so charismatic very swiftly created a highly critical atmosphere against him.

The change that followed was spectacular, and it is worth examination and analysis. Communications specialists provide us an explanation for this fatal change. This was given an appropriate tribute through a caricature of the individual in question on the Crackòvia comedy programme. An egocentric Laporta is satirised as a despot who enslaves his secretary, suffers from ridiculous ticks and is compulsively power-hungry.

Expressions such as 'Watch out!' or 'We aren't so bad!' have a special meaning in the annals of blue-red follies.

Confidence must be cultivated and preserved. That is one of Guardiola's strengths. He has common sense, and he communicates it in a credible manner. Everything is in flux and unmistakable.

And by all appearances, he has also infected his staff and players with this spirit. It is as if they were saying, 'Yes we can.'

(Obama's slogan could be seen on FC Barcelona posterns and banners after the Champions League victory in Rome. It was also rendered in modified versions such as 'Pep we can' or 'Yes we Pep.')

> *No efficient leader lacks credibility.*
> *Credibility is only possible when there is*
> *also trust. It is very difficult to gain trust,*
> *but it is easy to lose it.*

POST-VICTORY SCENERY

After FC Barcelona's impressive win against Athletic Bilbao at Mestalla Stadium on the evening of 14 May 2009, Guardiola and his assistant and friend Manuel Estiarte (the club's PR director) walked around alone on the completely empty pitch and spoke about what had occurred briefly before.

From one side, Pep could be seen gesticulating while Estiarte himself smiled in satisfaction. TV3 broadcasted these images but unfortunately omitted to hire a lip reader to decode the interesting words of this dialogue on the turf. Despite everything, Pep's gestures were unambiguous. Pep is an expressive person. This is a part of his charisma. His gestures were almost too masterfully imitated by the person who parodies him on Crackòvia.

Excellent work is not only free of boundaries. It also is not measured by regular working hours. Devotion is the most important condition for success. Pep has demonstrated numerous examples of this devotion, much unlike some of his predecessors who often made training into a relaxed and, needless to say, well-paid leisure activity.

Pep Guardiola did not promise to win any titles but said he would give it everything he had. 'The players will run tirelessly…' he said. And this is true. That is exactly what he achieved. The fruits of his first two seasons are textbook examples of how important it is simply to be there. One has to go out onto the pitch and control the scene. At the same time, we must constantly scrutinise our actions.

It is the continuous, almost compulsive, desire for improvement. It is the search for outstanding performance.

It makes little sense to apply the Guardiola method if this prerequisite is not fulfilled. We must dedicate all of our energy to what we want to achieve.

Work, work and more work. There is no other secret. There is also no other way. Those who attempt to avoid the task at hand should not count on Guardiola. The coach of the Catalan team has demonstrated this both actively and passively. The stories of Guardiola in which he is compulsively watching the games of his next opponent when the rest of the group is sleeping—whether in a bus or on a plane—are well known.

The numbers speak for themselves, and they do this in an impressive manner. Seven out of nine titles. Unbelievable.

Such fruit may only be harvested by those who have been chosen to win.

> *The Guardiola method is based on one*
> *absolute condition: absolute devotion*
> *to work. This, together with the young*
> *coach's proverbial common sense,*
> *form an anvil with which he forges his*
> *admirable success.*

THE DAY WHEN EVEN HE LOSES

Not long after winning the 2009 season title, the championship winning team flew to Mallorca. There they lost 1:2 to the home team on 16 May 2009 even though Eto'o made one goal and struck the goalpost with two other shots. One of them was even a penalty kick in the final minutes of the game.

Following the game, Guardiola called the usual press conference. One journalist congratulated him again on winning the title and asked him if he had already read the day's press releases.

'Yes, I'm familiar with them. Especially with what was written about the team.'

El País newspaper had dedicated the front page of its Sunday issue to him. It was a dedication to the best discovery of a new coach in the 2008-2009 La Liga season.

When Guardiola was asked about this, he said in all earnestness something that he had apparently considered very thoroughly.

'We won. Everyone is praising this victory. However, there will also be a day when we lose, and then it will be quite different. But I know how to lose; you'll see.'

Victory and defeat complete the circle. One cannot exist without the other. There can be no victory without the possibility of defeat.

This is a view that demonstrates an awareness of constant change as well as the flighty and transient nature of public opinion and those who form it: journalists.

To admit the possibility that there may not always be victories after winning is a great gesture. It speaks to the fact that this cycle has been visualised. It is an affirmation of profound knowledge of the fortuitousness of life and great maturity.

One can have no satisfaction without first experiencing pain.

The changing nature of things is the only thing that never changes.

Xavier Fuertes, currently the managing director of the Journalists Association of Catalonia, met Guardiola once in the cafeteria of an airport when they were both 25 years old. Barcelona had just been defeated 0:5. He asked Pep for an autograph for his wife and ventured to ask him,

'What do you do in such cases to avoid all of the pressure?'

Guardiola's response amazed him with its great maturity:

'I concentrate on myself. That enables me to avoid all of it because I know that it is only temporary.'

> *A good leader knows that all things change with one exception: the fact that everything changes.*

'A CLOCKWORK GUARDIOLA'

The plethora of names that have been given to Guardiola's Barça may be astonishing to many. It was especially intense during his first season. Giving a team a nickname also serves the purpose of keeping it in our minds. Incidentally, Barcelona has very creative fans in this regard.

We have yet to learn which name will actually stick with the team, but I would like to at least mention one I heard on Catalunya Ràdio during the Puyal programme on 17 May 2009. I found it quite amusing: 'A Clockwork Guardiola' derived from A Clockwork Orange. On one hand, the latter was the name bestowed upon the legendary Dutch national team, and on the other, it was the title of Stanley Kubrick's well-known film from the early 1970s. It was a film that characterised an entire generation, a virtually classic movie on violence in the urban social classes.

Which name would be best? In 2009, I would have voted for 'TriBarça Series 6:2'. I believe that the triple and the 6:2 win in Madrid were Guardiola's greatest successes during his first year coaching the team.

Before Pep had won the last title of the triple, my choices were 'GigaBarça, Series 6:2' and 'Peptium 2009 Processor'.

However, after Barça won the triple (which could not have happened more quickly), I felt I should probably think of something shorter and decided in favour of the simple 'TriBarça' to represent a team that holds triple value.

After the team has won four more titles (seven total), I would be in favour of 'Pep Team', as Pep is the deciding factor in this winning machine. Is it not so?

> *A good leader possesses the ability to change people and revive latent energies. The task is to add, add, add and then multiply, multiply, multiply.*

THE PENITENTS

When Guardiola was selected to coach the first squad, Catalan society erupted in a fiery debate between proponents and opponents of the choice.

Many of the latter saw Guardiola 'as a coach with a great future', but believed he would burn out prematurely, especially after president Laporta's controversial leadership of the club and all of the trouble caused by lack of confidence in him.

Thus, Guardiola took his new post under extremely difficult conditions. There was a president about whom there were many doubts, an angry fan base and another title-less season although the team had spent many game days at the top of the standings.

After the first successful season under Guardiola's leadership, many felt compelled to recognise that they had been mistaken and had falsely assessed the accomplishments and potential of the Catalan team's young coach.

Guardiola managed to do something quite remarkable. He engendered general acceptance and recognition. He was even able to achieve this with the mass media outlets, of which a few had already prepared the (sharpened) axe in order to make him a little shorter at his first failure even if he had been such a great symbol of 'Barcelonism' as a first-team player and an emblem of a very specific playing style.

There were penitents...and after some time they were queuing up to ask for absolution from Josep Guardiola who had been more or less beatified by the fans after the club experienced the two most successful seasons in its history.

Some fanatic supporters are said to have been overtaken by delirium and have seen the flawless visage of the lad from Santpedor in the shrine to the virgin Moreneta of Montserrat with a ball at the foot of the statue and adorned with up to seven cups. It was an absolutely heavenly icon for blue-red supporters and a society that had suffered so many misfortunes.

A leader persuades his supporters and critics through examples and counterexamples. In doing this, he proves his abilities and legitimises his claim to leadership.

Guardiola always has clear ideas. That is an important characteristic for a person who has dedicated himself to the task of leading a sports team.

*'If one does not know to which port one
is sailing, no wind is favourable.'*

Those are the words of a famous saying. It is a message of great importance for anyone who would like to take on leadership responsibilities.

When directing an organisation, it is absolutely necessary to know where one wants to go and have a strategy to follow in order to arrive there. The strategy is dependent on the objectives and not the other way round. This is a golden rule that every leader should always keep in mind.

Guardiola has always demonstrated crystal-clear ideas. In his first statements as coach, he made assurances that he felt well prepared for the task that he had taken on. *'If I weren't prepared, I wouldn't be standing before you here today,'* said Guardiola straightforwardly.

Guardiola communicated conviction, strength and optimism from the very beginning. The latter is a virtue that Barcelona fans have traditionally not possessed in abundance. In the past, the club's supporters were governed more by fear, the feeling of being the victims of an evil curse and a pathological sort of pessimism.

Guardiola was the antithesis to this inasmuch as he demonstrated a wonderful blend of optimism and caution. He had absolute confidence in his strengths, but experience had taught him enough to know that anything is possible on the pitch.

The fact that he lives with intensity and has been able to draw the right conclusions from this is one of the strengths of the Catalan coach's career.

What could one really tell him about the setbacks that fortune holds? What could be said about the misfortunes that suddenly leave one high and dry or about the rapid disappearance of friends and supporters when things do not go well?

The saying '*Victory has 100 fathers; defeat is an orphan*' is very fitting.

Pep has already had to deal with major setbacks. The idea of wanting to avoid these twists and turns would be just as laughable as imposing fines for excessive speed at the racetrack in Indianapolis.

Pep is a survivor, a gladiator and a man with a mission, and his hour came in the 2008-2009 season. The chosen one of the Catalan *Matrix* did not test fate by swallowing a blue or red pill. His pill was blue-red. And when he had taken the pill, he took over the wheel of the great ship and piloted it successfully to seven harbours.

> *A leader must feel a mission inside himself. He must be convinced that he has an objective to reach and that he has to utilise all of his ability and energy as well as that of those with him.*

WHAT IS A LEADER?

But what is a leader? I asked myself this question one day sitting in front of a computer screen in the Kennedy Presidential Library and Museum. I was there to read the outstanding speeches of the members of the clan of politicians whose name is borne by the aforementioned institution. One of these speeches contains the statement about defeat being an orphan.

There is no doubt that we also deem it proper to use that word to describe leaders in accordance with their competence. A leader's words must be capable of energising and stirring their audience. John F. Kennedy was a good example of this.

However, a leader is distinguished by much more than a mere ability to communicate. A leader has an entire portfolio of preferences and proven habits at his or her disposal as well as a distinct method of working.

In his significant work, *The Seven Habits of Highly Effective People,* North American author Stephen R. Covey (a great management visionary) detailed what a good leader must do in both his professional and personal lives. The latter also requires leadership and paradoxically can land those involved in precarious situations.

I am fully convinced that a person is essentially what he or she accomplishes. It is not enough to know what he or she thinks, thinks he or she is saying or thinks what he or she will say. It is also insufficient to know what he or she thinks he will do.

The ability to accomplish things is the true dimension that distinguishes a person.

The words of Confucius also leave no room for doubt in this regard:

> *'We can be touched by words, but only a good example carries us along.'*

Guardiola's actions are always consistent with his words. This is why his example carries us along. How? Well by minute yet major details such as these:

- He is the first to arrive at practice and often the last to leave.
- He analyses his opponents meticulously in order to identify weaknesses and strengths and act accordingly.
- He makes use of the expert staff he assembled himself.
- He conforms to the individual needs of each of his squad's players through the principles of coaching (i.e., he takes an individualised approach with each player).
- He is speaks to the press with disciplined regularity but does not break his self-imposed commitment and does not give journalists interviews outside of this framework.
- He works closely and confidently with his staff; however, he also establishes rules to hinder any information leaks.

- He praises his players in public and makes them into the actual protagonists of victories.
- He is always prepared to use internal communication to serve his players, their needs and concerns.

These are all habits that together represent a way of working and define a leadership style.

Clinical psychologist Antoni Bolinches says something very fitting in his epilogue when he ascertains that it is not so much that Guardiola has a method but rather that he 'is a method.' That means that the coach projects his personality, and every star and heavenly body on the team absorbs his light.

A CERTAIN

SAMUEL ETO'O

A CERTAIN
SAMUEL ETO'O ■ ■ ■

Samuel Eto'o, a great player from Cameroon, was Pep Guardiola's touchstone as a leader. Eto' o provides a good example of how to treat a person who is an outstanding player but also holds great conflict potential and at times displays an inflated ego and difficult character (with symptoms of bipolar disorder).

Many were of the opinion very early on that Eto'o should leave the club to avoid possible further incidents.

The big blue-red family was in agreement that the Cameroonian caused conflicts. This general opinion could also be heard over and over through July of 2009, as negotiations on his remaining in the club were underway.

Guardiola's behaviour was the key to his success in his first year. Pep initially took Eto'o out of the limelight but then reversed his decision, put him back on the team (no one else wanted to sign him) and ultimately even motivated him to play a fantastic season.

Through all of it, Guardiola stuck to the classic saying, 'Only wise people reverse decisions,' but he also displayed pragmatism, as the club's management was unable to part ways with the player in the end.

The Cameroonian was under constant pressure, and it was never clear when we would explode. Guardiola ultimately removed him from the team due to his lacking sense of belonging.'

A good leader is flexible and able to adapt. At the same time, he does not violate his own principles. Moreover, he has strategic abilities. There is a decision for every moment and a moment for every decision.

It is just as wrong to do things too early as it is to do them too late.

ETO'O: HONORIS CAUSA

I became acquainted with Samuel Eto'o when I was living in Mallorca and working as the communications director for the Riu Hotels & Resorts chain. I happened to run into him at a kiosk at Son Sant Joan Airport, as the same way I had met many other Mallorcan personalities. (I especially remember the day that I met renowned painter Miquel Barceló there. I initially took him for a beggar due to his slovenly clothing. In the end, we discussed the terrible consequences of malaria in Africa where he was returning to paint.)

In one of my run-ins with Eto'o, I revealed that I was a volunteer at the Campaner Foundation, which has dedicated itself to the fight against noma, a disease affecting undernourished children. I spent five years as the communications director of this non-government organisation (NGO). Noma distorts the faces of children and is often fatal. It is a dreadful disease but can be

easily treated with penicillin (more information at www.
fundacioncampaner.com).

I politely reminded Eto'o that he had not yet contributed
his donation of 6,000 Euros that he had promised us after
learning of a Nigerian girl suffering from this disease in
Son Dureta Hospital. Our Foundation was raising funds to
pay for her operation.

Samuel gave me his telephone number and asked me to
call him and remind of his promise.

The player initially showed me his beaming white
teeth and a distrustful facial expression that eventually
disappeared. In the end, he gave me a very pleasant smile.
I had experienced the good and compassionate Samuel.

However, I did have to move heaven and earth to obtain
the promised donation. Nonetheless, after countless calls
and with the support of other volunteers, we did it.

Even at that time, I noticed that the player was quite moody.
He could swiftly change his mind and was distrustful. A
large portion of this can perhaps be traced to his lack of
education. In the end, he held his word, and we were very
grateful to him for it.

When FC Barcelona signed a contract with him, we at
the Campaner Foundation thanked him publically for his
support. We then decided to use the opening of a seat of
our foundation in Barcelona (in the Journalists Association

International Press Centre building at 10 Rambla de
Cataluña) to announce him as a patron of our organisation.
We also wanted to invite the media to a public event to be
held on this occasion. That was in September of 2004.

Oddly enough, it was initially through the Campaner
Foundation that the blue-red public came to know the
supportive and compassionate Eto'o. It seemed only fitting
for us to recognise him publically. It was a good opportunity
to thank him for his donation and simultaneously announce
the official opening of our NGO in Catalonia.

We were fully aware that this was an ideal PR opportunity
for Samuel Eto'o, but he deserved it, at least at that time.

The player seemed mature, ready to concentrate on the
task before him and prepared to carry out his new public
role. This was the new Samuel, and we took great pride in
this fact. We believed in him.

With this sentiment in mind, we invited the mass media
to the event room at the International Press Centre in
Barcelona. To create a good visual image, I bought a
mortarboard (which cost me 6 Euros) at a nearby costume
shop (Mannikan, on Gran Vía) and a football, which the
player was to sign. The football would then be given to the
children at our facility in Niger.

As the hour of the ceremony approached, a great number
of journalists and photographers filled the conference hall.
The atmosphere in the room was impressive.

I called the player's agent, Josep Maria Mesalles, one last time to ensure that Eto'o would be there soon. After a somewhat awkward silence and after I reminded him that the room as about to burst at the seams, Mesalles assured me that they were both already on their way.

However, I only believed it when I saw them both enter the room. My gut told me something was off.

What would have happened if they had not come?

Eventually they entered the room. The player was smiling broadly, and his agent looked more baffled than anything else. They apologised for their late arrival saying they had been held up in traffic.

I remember the player's entry into the conference hall as one of the most intense journalistic moments of my life.

As it turned out, the journalists in attendance had very little interest for the Campaner Foundation or the problems of Africa. However, they were thrilled that I had honoured the player with a honoris causa mortarboard. This image subsequently appeared on the front pages of the sporting press, in the sports sections of newspapers and in news programmes.

The photo and television cameras also latched on to the autographed ball for the children in Niger. They had an image and a headline: Eto'o's compassionate face despite his controversial past. Everything went like clockwork.

Everyone was happy and content. Even Mr. and Mrs. Campaner (Pep and Marilena) were impressed by the vast amount of media in attendance at the ceremony.

The whole event ended up lasting longer than planned, and several media representatives then tried to get personal interviews. Both Eto'o and his agent looked somewhat exhausted by that time.

I especially remember the poor manners of one veteran reporter from a private television company who absolutely wanted to have his own photos. He did not have the slightest interest in the event's poster even if that was also a golden opportunity.

The poster in question announced the presence of a new foundation in Catalonia dedicated to saving starving children in Africa.

It was my first glimpse at the lack of human qualities in some sports journalists. I later observed other examples of how perfidiously the press can treat media stars and starlets who hold their interest. There is a type of journalism that has nothing to do with the principle of truth and offers a cocktail of subservience and extreme nepotism for both sides in a way that contradicts the very spirit of athletics.

It was a profound but necessary disappointment. Things are the way they are.

('You are absolutely right, Miguel Angel.' I hear an imaginary voice in my head that speaks to me with an intonation similar to that of the expert Domènec Balmanya, renowned radio reporter José María García's eternal lackey.)

> *Sports are a good thing—*
> *sports journalism is quite often not.*

SAMUEL AT 26,000 FEET

The day after Samuel Eto'o's appointment as the foundation's patron, I took the midday Spanair flight from Barcelona to Palma de Mallorca. I had already read the day's papers and cut out certain articles. I was feeling good. To make things even better, the airline surprised me with a free upgrade to business class. As they say, it was a good day.

The cabin doors were about to be shut when one last passenger entered the business-class area and, at the flight attendant's instruction, took the seat next to me. He was dressed like a teenager and wearing large headphones.

'Samuel!'

It was actually him. Samuel Eto'o, the patron honoris causa. We were sitting in the same airplane to Mallorca. I greeted him effervescently and immediately showed him what I had cut out of the day's papers. He looked through everything with interest. He read attentively without noticing my comments and became fully lost in himself.

Then he looked at me earnestly and said,

'The journalists have no fucking idea about football.'

He was referring to certain commentaries assuring that he was not fit without taking into consideration that he had missed all of pre-season prep. His face reflected scarcely concealed rage. This was the angry, barely controllable and terrifying Samuel.

We spoke for a while longer, and I asked him,

'Will so much excitement, so much applause not change your character someday? Will you always remain supportive and compassionate as well?'

Samuel looked at me steadily and replied,

'Miguel Angel, I will never change. I will always remain the same.'

The coming months were to become a clear contradiction of this statement made at 26,000 feet over the Mediterranean on that beautiful September day.

The player's co-operation with the Campaner Foundation, which had opened all of its doors to him upon his arrival in Barcelona, was dropped entirely without any explanation whatsoever.

In contrast, Eto'o devoted himself to an ever-increasing number of public appearances with all sorts of NGOs. He did this without batting an eye and fully aware that he was substantially improving his image in the eyes of potential sponsors while his past as a contentious player slipped gradually into oblivion.

We had nothing to say about this. Those who call for solidarity with their own cause must also grant it to others. However, we gradually began to perceive the oddity of how he ignored us. He showed no interest whatsoever, stopped supporting us publically and offered no support although many mass media outlets still associated the Campaner Foundation's mission with his name, a perception that had come to be anything but accurate. He made no claims, but he did not deny anything either. He was simply using us.

Eventually, we felt compelled to write to the player's agent, Josep Maria Mesalles, and express our disappointment to him.

His response was dreadful, impolite, unrestrained and written in poor language. It demonstrated a sort of cynicism that hurt us deeply.

There is no question that people in the public eye may draw benefits from their good deeds, but such actions should be carried out in a loyal and consistent manner. One should not reap the benefits of merits unearned.

Eto'o's image with the foundation fell through the floor. We pondered whether we should hang the poster of him in the bedrooms of our fosterlings in Niger, but how could we explain this to them? We did not want to make them suffer unnecessarily and refrained from this thought. We gradually forgot the whole affair as the day-to-day operations of an NGO are stressful enough in themselves.

In the meantime, a representative of the player was speaking to the media about fantasy joint projects. This false cynicism really nettled us.

Eto'o ultimately announced his withdrawal from the foundation after a long conversation between the organisation's founder and Eto'o's lawyer.

Was it out of a guilty conscience? Because he wanted to repair a little of the damage? Was it a well-intended gesture? I do not know. Time will tell, and that also goes for the true dimension of his social projects here in Spain and in other parts of the world including his own country of Cameroon.

These feigned supportive attitudes taught me much. I no longer believe in anything that I cannot verify with my own eyes when it comes to solidarity and charity. My level of scepticism has become astronomic.

In contrast, I now value more than ever all campaigns (even if they are quite small) that are carried out effectively and without attracting a lot of attention. These are efforts that above all benefit those close to home without dedicating themselves to exotic projects on multiple continents or constantly striving for media attention.

They are something you do simply because your conscience tells you that you should do something.

There were all sorts of events surrounding Samuel Eto'o in the years that followed. There were speculations about him staying with Barça, his transfer to Inter Milan, angry press statements and constantly changed decisions. However, this is not the place for that. It all only serves as proof of how money dominates everything. It pollutes and poisons. That is simply how football works.

I prefer the image of the kind pleasant Samuel who was leafing through newspapers at the airport in Palma and wanted to help the poor girl in Africa. His intentions were good then. They came from the heart. He remembered how he himself had come to Madrid as a boy without a penny to his name or anyone to support him.

That is the Samuel that I would like to remember.

The subsequent development of his personality deserves no admiration in my eyes. That also goes for his exhibition of luxury in general (cars, watches, female companions) and his aggressive nuances in a world so in need of peace. All of this has no value whatsoever. What counts is a good heart and compassion as he displayed as our patron in good times, the Eto'o who was simply Samuel.

> *Sports offer great opportunities to assume social responsibility, but they also attract people who abuse this.*

ON THE IMPORTANCE

OF ROLE MODELS

ON THE IMPORTANCE
OF ROLE MODELS ■ ■ ■

Over the course of my professional career as a management consultant, I have had the opportunity of becoming acquainted with a vast array of organisations. Of all them, a certain type especially stood out: those with leaders who led by example.

It is not enough to organise costly seminars on internal communication (of which I have also led many), write the best handbooks in the world (paper is patient) or make announcements of all sorts concerning what will happen if such measures are not accompanied by exemplary daily behaviour.

The personality of an organisation is initially formed after the role model it sees on a daily basis. Values become deep convictions and automatic processes that make work easier in everyday life. It is exactly this and nothing else that creates the magic energy, which circulates in the nervous system of an organisation.

It is said that words and actions are two different things. A leader cannot appear credible without setting the example. A manager cannot motivate his organisation without being involved in it. No one will identify with a higher mission without internal communications. It does not matter what is at stake: seven titles, semi-annual sales increases, reducing complaints due to lack of materials or reducing illness-related absences.

Now I would like to tell a few stories. When I was working for the Riu Hotel chain (1996-2008), I was astonished that their co-founder, Lluís Riu Bertran, always asked for the worst room when visiting his company's hotels.

I asked him why he did this, and his clever answer was as follows:

'For a start, I do not want one of my guests to get the worst room. If I myself am in the worst room, I can see what needs to be done for it to become a good room.'

In this regard, he was the typical sort of managing director who also picked up bits of paper lying on the hallway carpet of his hotels. He did not direct others to do this. He did it himself.

It would not hurt any director or deputy director to follow this example. When the highest-ranking officer sets the route of march, you follow it. When the co-founder set a good example, why would his employees not follow it?

Role models can obviously motivate people. It is not enough to do this with words alone. Being available at all times demands comprehensive abilities and complete devotion to the task at hand. One must be vigilant at all times and never grow tired, and, if possible, never flirt with stress. It is a worthy goal.

When one is capable of persuading a group of people of the value of a mission they have to accomplish and are capable of fulfilling, they form an unstoppable force.

That is exactly what Pep Guardiola has managed to do.

> *A leader is only credible if he leads by example. No leader can motivate others without personal involvement.*

THE LEADER AS AN INSPIRER

Time and again I return to Boston for study and research purposes. While there in early 2009, I came upon a series of editorials at Harvard University's Cooperative Society that dealt with the topic of leaders as inspirers. According to expert opinion, these leaders are people capable of establishing an emotional bond with their protégés.

There is no doubt whatsoever that a good leader must possess the ability to guide emotions. Correctly channelled emotions can enable us to accomplish wonderful things. Incorrectly channelled emotions can lead to absolute catastrophes.

The term *emotional intelligence* was coined over fifteen years ago. It is a concept that has been very successful because of a book by North American journalist Daniel Goleman.

The author claims that the key to a balanced and effective life lies in the ability to understand the emotions of others.

If there's one thing that football is, it is a veritable circus of emotions. It is a circus fuelled above all by the communications media, which have discovered an incomparable source of income in the game with the ball.

I may be a romantic, but I still remember the times (in the 1970s) when the commercialisation of sports was still less apparent. It goes without saying that the pros have the right to become wealthy just as the media are authorised to conduct their business. However, the sports-profit binomial has a perverse dimension that is worth taking a closer look at.

Football plays with people's emotions and feelings. However, the person who truly controls the competition is a lord of armies.

When this is transferred to the field of journalism, it becomes clear that the truth is in no way the greatest value. The most important thing of all is the show. This leads to violations of every possible ethic principle in the book.

There is a simple reason for this. A massive amount of money is at stake, and that infects everything.

> *The truth is no longer the ultimate goal in many fields of journalism.*

IT IS QUITE SIMPLE—AFTER ALL, WE CALL IT COMMON SENSE

In seeking to find the reasons for Guardiola's success, there is one term that invariable comes to mind: common sense.

Well what is common sense, this virtue that appears to be so deeply rooted in Catalan society?

Years ago when I was still doing my *Notes interiors* programme as part of *El suplement on Catalunya Ràdio*, I asked myself what this expression actually means. I even asked myself if it was a sign of good common sense to want to define this term.

There have been various opportunities thus far that have given me occasion to write about common sense and thoroughly analyse this concept. Common sense is better viewed as an exceptional human sense.

Here are some of my thoughts on common sense: They have something to do with logic when it comes to actions. It is a logic based on the ordinary, the collective and people in general.

In this regard, common sense deals with the predictability of behaviour patterns. It has to do with putting oneself in another's position in order to predict their reactions and foresee how events will develop based on similar or comparable experiences.

Common sense thus refers to collective knowledge, a sort of state-of-the-art logic of our environment. It is a matter of predicting human reactions. It has something to do with reaping what one sows. Hence, in a certain way, it refers to morals, the happy medium and the responsibility that we all have to our neighbour.

Pep Guardiola applies common sense in practice. If you want to create a true team, its components must know each other inside and out. That is why he started his initiative of having his players eat together and socialise. This also allowed him to monitor whether their eating habits were consistent with those of professional athletes.

(For example, that is how Guardiola learned that Messi had never eaten fish. He prescribed him a diet free of both popcorn and pizza, and he has not injured himself since.)

It is also very sensible to promote the consumption of fruit by serving it peeled, making it easier to eat. This is now common practice in Barça training units.

What is actually astonishing is that these fundamental things had not been done much earlier (we are talking about pros who are millionaires in a world-class club). It is surprising that the professionalisation of the team had not advanced very far and that it took a meticulous coach to introduce these new conventions. In doing this, he also applied much of what he had learned in Italy.

(The practices of a coach from Sevilla should also be mentioned here. He checks the quality of mattresses to establish which ones his players will sleep on best.)

> *Common sense has something to do with the logic of the collective, with people. It implies putting oneself in another's position when it comes to taking decisions.*

INSTILLING TRUST

One of Guardiola's first controversial measures was to do away with pre-home game training camps and travel into the city from the suburbs on game days.

Any football fan knows that the idea behind training camps (which the players absolutely abhor) is to monitor a number of dietary habits and resting phases during the crucial hours before a game.

In contrast, Pep puts his confidence in the players and demonstrates that he trusts them. They should monitor these things themselves. Of course, this approach does have certain risks, but it also saves the worry of a great many control measures.

This trust obviously has limits. There are a number of internal rules that must be observed, such as arriving at practice on time and being home by a certain time.

Public opinion has already realised how strict Pep Guardiola can be when it comes to fining players who arrive at practice only a minute late. This is surely an intelligent approach by the coach.

This could also be construed as excessive or eccentric behaviour. However, it is exactly the opposite. The secret of punctuality is not in showing up at a particular location on time but actually in arriving there before the time specified. This time buffer provides a certain measure of security for coping with unforeseen circumstances.

When I held press conferences over the years for the Riu hotel chain in Madrid, journalists invariably arrived late with the argument, *'The traffic in Madrid was especially bad today.'* Not true! Traffic was always bad. They should have left early enough to account for that.

Punctuality is also an issue of decency and setting a good example when it comes to creating a certain culture within a group.

This is why Guardiola introduced a system in which punctuality was given high priority. By doing this, he intimated to his players that all were equal before the rules and that there would be no exceptions.

> *Being punctual is a way of expressing*
> *the importance we ascribe to what we do*
> *and the people with whom we work.*

RECOLLECTIONS OF

RONALDINHO & DECO?

RECOLLECTIONS OF RONALDINHO & DECO? ■ ■ ■

Even during the tenure of Rijkaard, Guardiola's predecessor on the coach's bench, Deco from Portugal caused the most dressing-room conflicts. Ronaldinho subsequently proved himself Deco's worthy successor in the next season. He was capable of interrupting an entire training session because he wanted a bottle of Coca-Cola.

It's almost too laughable to put it nicely.

In Ronaldinho's case, one must differentiate between two phases. During the first, he was a hardworking player, and in the second, he became completely addicted to an excessive lifestyle.

Neither investigative journalism nor detectives were required to establish this fact. In reality, one needed only to learn a little bit about the nightlife scene in Castelldefels.

The regression of a pro of Ronaldinho's class is one of the saddest episodes in the history of FC Barcelona. How could it be permitted for a player who was the basis of the entire playing system in such a demanding high-performance sport as professional football to decide in favour of the *Dolcefarniente*?

Coach Rijkaard's lack of responsibility in this context stands in contrast to his first two seasons characterised by effective and precise leadership.

Coach Rijkaard's football project collapsed the day that Ronaldinho replaced attending daily practice with evening fitness centre workouts (in actuality he was sleeping off his high). There is nothing worse in an organisation than unequal treatment. Ronaldinho demanded this, and the blue-red side suffered the inevitable for two seasons.

It was a valuable lesson of which Guardiola took careful notice.

What became of Ronaldinho and Deco? After putting FC Barcelona behind them, they accomplished little of note in football, and their behaviour caused remarkable damage to their own prestige.

It is highly irritating—as in the case of Ronaldinho or even Maradona—when the very players that are admired by children fail to live up to the expectations that they have awakened in them. We need role models with certain behaviour patterns. When the chosen few fail in this regard, the repercussions cause grave damage to society.

This was also the case with Argentine player Diego Armando Maradona. His skills as a player were beyond reproach. He is one of the best footballers of all time. However, his cynicism and the negative development of his personality would be welcome in any chamber of horrors as an example of how a main character in an anti-drug advertising campaign gives in fully to his own cocaine addiction.

These were painful episodes, and they must not be forgotten. We cannot simply turn a blind eye to them as some try to do. It was a very dark chapter in football history. There are always groups of alleged friends who are eager help the big stars dig their own grave.

In light of this lamentable spectacle, one misses a critical press that tells things the way they are. I mean a press free of commercial interests that explains point by point how the great figures of football (that they put on a pedestal) are sliding deeper and deeper into moral decline.

Freedom of the press? Don't make me laugh. The only freedom that truly exists is the freedom to distribute towels, swimming trunks, slippers, bathrobes and all sorts of other items with the club's logo on them. It is a big business in which the most important factor is missing: a detailed explanation of what is actually happening.

> *Great players can provide examples of exemplary behaviour, but they can also do the exact opposite.*

FOOTBALL AND CORRUPTION

Let's not deceive ourselves. Football is a business that reeks of corruption. The magnitude of mutual interests, buccaneers that use every opportunity for personal gain, the ever-present middlemen …

And unfortunately all of this is happening in an environment in which corruption is widely tolerated.

The shameless spectacle at the close of every season shows us how taken pro football is with the mercenary mentality. There can be no objections to players attempting to gain

higher salaries, but these proclamations of inviolable love for the colours of their clubs only lead to embarrassment for the proclaimers in the long run.

The passion surrounding the game of football is so strong that improper behaviour, attempts at emotional extortion and commercial pressure of all kinds are simply ignored in a steady stream of buying and selling teaming with legions of intervening middlemen.

When it comes to player signings, we have the same inevitable moments of suspicion that surface time and again regarding those responsible for making purchases in major companies. Both are hot on the trail of poorly hidden kickbacks. If we had real investigative journalism in our country, stories would come to light that would make even the most stoic among us flush crimson with shame.

You can learn all about that from people who know exactly what they're talking about if you promise not to use their name. That goes for high-ranking journalists as well as executive board members who have had the opportunity to participate directly in various negotiations.

Let's be honest. Corruption blossoms and spreads its tentacles in places where a lot of money is at stake and flowing swiftly.

> *The power of money poisons the purity*
> *of feelings. Football abounds with one*
> *and the other: both money and feelings.*

DESPITE EVERYTHING, THERE ARE VALUES

At this point, one might argue, 'Well, what is the sense of talking about values?' My response: It makes absolute sense. It is especially appropriate to speak out in favour of clear and sportsmanlike values in our materialistic and vain environment and to use them as a winning strategy.

I am firmly convinced that FC Barcelona's latest season has had the best advertising impact thus far for Catalonia and Catalans throughout Spain and abroad.

I receive many testimonies of admiration for Pep Guardiola. They come from simple people on the street, academics, people in leadership positions and opinion-makers in Madrid. His actions, his abilities and his elegance have captured countless people.

Many would be happy to be in our position. We managed an entire series of clear victories. They were earned and won with decency without any sort of sporting violence or obscure tactics. They were gained in a spirit of openness, a home-grown way of playing and with risky football that sought to be attractive. In doing this, we tested our luck, respected our opponents at all times, accepted defeat and knew how to win. We dominated both sides.

I refuse to believe that one's achievements serve only as mass entertainment and have no moral, social or ideological repercussions whatsoever.

I refuse to believe that the success on the pitch that we had the pleasure of experiencing did not communicate a social, lasting and exhilarating message.

I refuse to believe that we are incapable of reflecting the leadership values, to which we owe the recent years of an attractive, admirable, winning and exemplary FC Barcelona.

THE METHOD IS A SUM OF ATTITUDES AND BEHAVIOURS

When asked if there is such thing as the Guardiola method, Pep answered in the negative.

'What there is, is a great many players.'

He was right. However, there is also a great coach.

There is no Guardiola method in the sense of a practical set of guidelines. There is no Guardiola method to be had as a set of measures for conducting training and developing an all-around effective game plan.

When we speak of the Guardiola method, we are referring to an entire series of attitudes which in turn reflect values.

These are values that can be applied to any organisation. They are values that hold the potential for success as they are based on respect for others and the firm belief in the culture of personal effort.

As psychologist Antoni Bolinches very aptly writes in his epilogue to this book, the Guardiola method is Guardiola

himself. Destiny has given us something that is almost a miracle. There is a person among us—close enough to touch—that knew how to develop a success strategy based on values we know.

These are values that stem from Catholicism and other religious beliefs, our social life, our customs and conventions, the examples set by our grandparents and generations of enterprising people who created an industrial sector. They also emanated from companies that

gave everything they had to close successful deals, travel, be proactive, trade and leave a mark on other places. Such enterprises demonstrate sensitivity for our culture, love our Catalan language and work to ensure that it is never lost regardless of who is in power...

All of this is the Guardiola method summarised in a code of values, which has proven exceedingly fruitful.

> *Leaders with good values systems achieve good results. Their teachings can be applied in every area imaginable.*

THE ARRIVAL OF CRISTIANO RONALDO: REAL MADRID TAKES A DIFFERENT PATH

JULY 2009

The big day for the fans of Real Madrid has arrived. The new idol Cristiano Ronaldo (96 million Euros—the price of the transfer speaks for itself) is to be presented to a packed Santiago-Bernabéu Stadium. Just as with a great initiation ritual, the masses have come to hail their saviour.

Real president Florentino Pérez watches the show from the stands with a smile on his face. His dream has come true. The next season has not yet begun, and the fans are already trembling in anticipation as they do on the afternoons of great victories. It is a drumbeat heard around the world.

Before Cristiano Ronaldo's arrival, we are flooded with an abundance of pleasant details on the Portuguese star player: his humble origins on the island of Madeira, his brother's drug addiction, his fighting spirit, his training diligence, his absolute calling to the game of football, his winner's mentality, his resolve…

An entire PR machine is in operation to obliterate the poor image of a moody and unpleasant Cristiano, an exceptionally aggressive player who makes primitive remarks and has poor manners, who is offensive and wasteful…

It is an impressive production. Almost 1,000 journalists have been accredited for the event. The people lust after a spectacle. This sort of thing feeds the whole world, the club, the football industry, the players and the sports media…

The show is financed by the masses. The only thing they ask in return is an emotional reward: goals in the stadium, feats of athletic heroism and the opportunity to look down on the fans of the opposing side.

That is how things work in football.

> *Football is financed by the masses. What do they receive in return? An emotional reward.*

Cristiano Ronaldo's first season with Real Madrid ends in a sports fiasco. After 250 million Euros had been invested in the side, it loses to the team from Alcorcón in the Spanish Cup, exits the Champions League quarterfinals after a loss to Olympique Lyonnais and ultimately takes second place behind Barça, which amasses an unbelievable 99 points.

President Florentino reacts. He fires coach Pellegrini and signs a coach who is the current rage: Jose Mourinho who had won the 2010 Champions League cup with Inter Milan.

President Florentino launches a new ambitious project. It is the next one in Florentino's era that remains true to a motto sarcastically called 'Cartera contra cantera' (Money for talent). Time will tell.

GUARDIOLA'S

ABSENCE

GUARDIOLA'S
ABSENCE ■ ■ ■

In July of 2009, there was one recurrent theme in sports reporting: Pep Guardiola's absence. Well, he was on vacation, but he was missed. Doesn't it seem odd?

The club president took advantage of Guardiola's absence to gain attention after remaining out of the limelight throughout the season as part of his 'low-profile' strategy. The season had produced a conveyor belt of victories, and the coach had become the true representative of the club.

President Laborta missed a great opportunity… to simply keep silent. His explanations did not serve the club in any way. In a time of collective jubilation, Laporta's statements were dripping with *madriditis*, a term for the pathological compulsion to occupy oneself with Real Madrid. And there we have them again: the complexes. They are exactly the opposite of what the Guardiola method prescribes: be strong and show respect.

Guardiola's development also shed light on president Laporta's weaknesses as a leader. There is a big difference in their mindsets as well as something that fundamentally separates the two: credibility. Guardiola has a great deal of it; Laporta, in contrast, holds significantly less. Sound leadership without full credibility does not exist. Laporta's statements against the 'imperialism' of Real Madrid were especially unfortunate. They signified a return to the darkest chapters of previous club president Nunez's tenure when vilification of the opponent was used as a diversion to distract from the club's own weaknesses.

The summer of 2009 cannot really be described as exemplary. Ecstatic with winning the championship, many Barcelona fans asked themselves if it had really just happened a few weeks ago. The sequence of unpleasant events made it seem as if much more time had passed.

> *It is impossible to lead others without solid credibility.*

THE ESSENCE OF THINGS

Let's put it this way: If we forget about the whole media circus surrounding the game of football and deal strictly with the essence of things, we see that 2009 and 2010 were something very special, a part of our lives that FC Barcelona fans must never forget. On the contrary, we must draw practical lessons from this experience. They were seasons that should be taught in school.

Some may believe these are the sort of isolated successes that football rewards you every now and then, that this is nothing to philosophise about and that you should simply stand tall and blissfully pile it all in your treasure chest of favourite memories.

Nothing is further from my intentions than to derive scientific lessons or irrefutable laws from this game. However, I firmly believe that the 2008-2009 seasons left us a legacy, a whole set of values and values systems that produce success. They are directives that we should internalise as if they were written in a compendium of examples of good style.

What I mean is having one's own style. All of the marketing experts continually reference how important it is to make yourself stand out, to remove yourself from the group and to position yourself as the best in a very specific manner when faced with the impossibility of being the best.

FC Barcelona created its own style. Its roots lie in the Dutch school that has also created great footballers in addition to great painters.

Pep Guardiola soaked up this tradition introduced by Johan Cruyff, refined it and served it to us on a platter as an immaculate sports delicacy.

Not every team cultivates its own style or its own behaviours. It is a special sort of capital that should be protected, an immaterial value that has something to do with one's own identity.

And that is also why it is a source of profound existential satisfaction.

Guardiola established his own style guide that serves the objective of achieving the extraordinary.

WHERE DOES THIS ENERGY COME FROM?

The month of May in 2009 was of crucial importance to the outcome of the season. Everything was at stake for the team. One of the greatest fears was that they would eventually reach the point when their strength would fail them. It was felt that they might not pull through in the moment of truth, and the season, which had been brilliant up to that point, would end in a fiasco.

During this terribly important month, a player, Xavi, gave an interview in which he said several things that were not initially noticed but provide a very precise description of many of the Catalan team's success factors.

In response to a question about whether the players would gradually come to feel a certain level of fatigue, he said,

'No, not at all. We feel better than ever. You should see how we train behind closed doors. We have more energy than ever before. We could run many of our plays blindfolded. If there were a camera that could show it, you would be speechless at what we are capable of...'

Energy is the key factor for an important task. What is the magic mechanism for regenerating it?

There is no doubt that the motivation for what we do is a very important source of energy. This energy drives us onward and allows us to forget our fatigue. It enables us to jump out of bed in the morning. It gives us vitality and yearning and ultimately fills us with joy in what we do.

This joy is easy to recognise. It can be seen as soon as you enter a place of work. It is immediately visible whether a place is charged with energy or suffering from an energy deficit. These are the vibrations that once senses directly.

Energy and a good mood are contagious but so are sadness and pessimism.

Guardiola and his staff have built a team that radiates positivity. It is a group in which people are full of energy every single day and where conflicts (which there have been) are not hung up for everyone to see but resolved internally and without involving more people than necessary.

Working with joy and a positive attitude
is the longest lasting energy source of all.

OVERCOMING CONFLICTS

Those who think the FC Barcelona dressing room has been a place of peace and quiet over that last two seasons are sorely mistaken. There have been conflicts and disputes here same as with all teams in any era. However, the major difference has been in the actual dimensions of the problems in question and the coach's ability to deal with them discretely while maintaining a just and balanced approach.

There is nothing worse for the harmony of a group than the unequal treatment that occurs when one individual receives a warning for a misstep while another gets off scot-free in the same situation.

Players are (young) people who constantly compare themselves to others, and they do this in every way possible. They compare clothes, cars, salaries and the brands for which they advertise.

In professional football club dressing rooms, the players are constantly analysing what is being said about the others. No detail is left untouched, but the opposite *('I haven't read the newspapers this week.')* is often claimed in order to hide the truth. Of course they read everything but didn't really like what was written.

Guardiola's demand that the new FC Barcelona sports centre in Sant Joan Despí be opened in order to concentrate all activities there was a clever strategic move from the point of view of the team's everyday work.

The prevalent pressure from society and the inability to escape it was one of the worst conflicts confronting the team. The constant requests for autographs, photos and proposals of all sorts…all of this puts the players off balance, and, even worse, it can warp their sense of reality.

The transition to Sant Joan Despí gave the side the opportunity to train in a quieter environment. The facilities were also better suited for the players to socialise with one another, and this is fundamental in developing team spirit.

Moreover, the team now has a regulation-sized pitch on which to train. This is an elementary condition that they previously did not have.

> *There are fewer conflicts, and when they do occur, they are better resolved in an ergonomic working environment (according to the activity in question) and without involving more people than necessary.*

PREDILECTION FOR DETAIL

One small detail can be crucial to winning in sports with intense competitive pressure (of which there is an increasing number in our modern times). The term *small detail* is not a reference to something incidental. A small detail can become a very substantial detail, and it can be of decisive importance when it arises.

For this reason, it is absolutely necessary to pay attention to the small details. They can make the difference.

The goals that FC Barcelona gained from standard situations during the first season under Guardiola's leadership are a good example of the fruits borne by small details. There were not many of them, but they were worth their weight in gold. They were the result of countless experiments behind closed doors where plays are studied with the intent of catching the opposing defence of guard.

This is often a matter of altering player positioning in order to take advantage of opponent weaknesses. In the run-up to the match, this requires much observation, consideration and the right analysis of the information gained.

Pep Guardiola is not a prototype footfall fanatic who watches game videos around the clock. He is an experienced user of what is known as the *benchmarking* technique. This term is used to describe the practice of imitating the best. Guardiola deals with the state of the art, the top level that he finds on the pitch. He applies the lessons that he draws from this experience, and when possible, attempts to take it one step further.

This inclination toward sniffing out innovations and applying them to everyday work is a distinguishing feature of the Barcelona trainer. He also knows how to surround himself with a group of recognised experts, a team of specialists representing the most varied disciplines.

This shows us the team's double dimension brought to life by Guardiola. On one hand, we have a sworn team of players whose will and talent are fully oriented towards a very specific objective, and on the other, we have a team of specialists who discretely and effectively resolve all of the problems of the dressing room.

A dressing room full of elite footballers is a microcosm, a world of its own. Of course, they are only people, but they have very special characteristics, are of different ages, come from various cultures and, very importantly, have different levels of maturity.

In this regard, the coach has a monumental task before him. He has to talk a lot (including one-on-one conversations), exchange views and adjust his approach to the needs of others.

An important trump card that Guardiola can play off of is that he was also once a player. That is why he understands exactly what is going on in his players' minds and knows when he has to give pointers and when it makes more sense to not intervene.

This was also an important feature made possible by Johan Cruyff during his tenure. He made it possible to be efficient as a coach. Even though his style was very different than Guardiola's, Cruyff always had an advantage. He was able to put himself in the mindset of his players, understand what moved them and then use this knowledge for the good of the team.

This ability to put oneself in the position of others is what psychologists call empathy. It is a very important virtue. Those who possess empathy are at an advantage when it comes to understanding problems, avoiding conflicts or steering these things in a particular direction without letting it get out of hand.

In many ways, Pep Guardiola had a great mentor in Johan Cruyff in terms of player management. Guardiola has actually never suffered from a lack of people in his life who inspired him.

In sports with extreme competitive pressure, the small details make the difference.

> *Empathy is the ability to place oneself in the position of others. It is an absolutely necessary virtue if one wants to resolve conflicts in a prudent manner.*

THE CONSTANT DESIRE TO KNOW MORE

There is one thing that attracts special attention when we study Guardiola's biography. He has a craving to know more, read more and hear more. Our protagonist possesses a great deal of intellectual curiosity that was not accompanied by a structured, let us say, academic, education.

The love of books is a characteristic feature and a key component of his nature as an analyst, strategist and keen observer with an inclination towards perfectionism. He has all of this in combination with extreme altruism.

In books on and interviews with Guardiola, he is always described as a person who always wants to know more. He wants to soak up everything, to gain the essence and to stand next to the great masters of football. He wants to hear their points of view, exchange opinions, have intense conversations, remove doubts and create new ones.

His public treatment of his teachers is simply outstanding. He is an extremely teachable student who sees every commentary as an opportunity for improvement.

An example of this is the book titled *La meva gent, el meu futbol (My People, My Football)*, which was written by players with the support of journalist Miguel Rico. This book provides insight into Guardiola's take on the people in football who formed him and left their mark on him.

He has a friendly word for everyone. In the worst of all cases, he maintains respectful silence. This also goes for Van Gall, author of one of the worst acts in Guardiola's eyes. In one of the darkest chapters in the last twenty years of the club's history, he was responsible for the firing of Guillermo Amor, a symbol of the work of the La Masía youth academy.

This appreciation for his teachers, for the people close to him, demonstrates a profound sort of gratitude that has nothing to do with any PR talent the coach may have.

This gratitude is something that has characterised his entire career. It found its highest form of expression when he said,

'My players are wonderful. I would be nothing without them.'

> Guardiola soaks up knowledge from any source and recognises the greatness of all who were at one time responsible for him.

A TEAM, A SUBJECTIVE CONDITION

How important is a coach to a team's success? Is it enough to have a large and strong squad? Is the importance of players overestimated?

At a luncheon in 2009 with FC Barcelona vice president Sandro Rosell, who would go on to be elected club president on 13 June 2010, I asked him these questions, and I received a clear answer.

'The coach plays only a secondary role in a team's success.'

Such an answer from a person who knows the football world so well surprised me. I have always believed the opposite. Although coaches do not shoot any goals, the goals are made possible by how they lead the group and get the best out of the players.

One of my most important examples of this is Spanish National Team coach Vincente del Bosque. In his first term as the president of Real Madrid, Florentino Pérez fired him because he found him too drab. It was a glaring error because the coaches who came later were in no way superior to him. Without del Bosque, Real Madrid won fewer titles. It may be that del Bosque was drab, but he created the conditions for the group to use their talent for the good of the team.

I am of the opinion that companies (and the country in general) are fundamentally a type of subjective condition. Those who are capable of creating a balanced state of mind are good team leaders. Those who cannot communicate this positive attitude will not be able to lead people to achieve great success.

Without contesting the team's technical skills or the excellent quality of several of its members, I refuse to believe that all of this could be achieved. A season is long and intense. There are constant causes for friction. Who is responsible for ensuring that these people are content? Without a doubt, the coach. That is where the results come from.

> *A leader must create the conditions that allow all of the talent of those in his charge to blossom. To a great extent, he is also responsible for their satisfaction.*

GUARDIOLA

FOR PRESIDENT?

GUARDIOLA FOR PRESIDENT? ■ ■ ■

Let's talk about the future.

In discussing the future, there are people who predict what will occur without saying when, or they say when but do not specify what.

However, I would like to speak about both in concrete terms. Will Pep Guardiola aspire to the presidency of FC Barcelona in the next 10 years? Will Guardiola become the Catalan version of Franz Beckenbauer, the great FC Bayern star who became president of the club?

It would be conceivable for a coach who has already won seven titles to raise the bar a little.

Does Pep Guardiola have the profile to be a suitable candidate for the FC Barcelona presidency?

My answer is unequivocal. Yes, the values that the young coach has exercised in both seasons can be easily applied to the demands of such a high office as those of the FC Barcelona president.

These are values that can be applied to any sport. Furthermore, Guardiola is an outstanding representative of his homeland. He is a Catalan to the core, judiciously passionate, fully identified with the colours of the club, devoted to the culture in which he was raised, bears a typical Catalan name and has an excellent public image.

Yes, he could be a great president…if he wanted to. One aspect that should be taken into consideration is that Guardiola is good when he does the things that he likes to do and has room to operate. He has to feel at ease in the role he plays. He would have a full decade to prepare for this role. He has already long since demonstrated his willingness to give it his all as well as his ability to develop a team and respect his opponents. Of all of the sports, Football is most often at the centre of attention. It is the most complex and important sport. It is a subject in which he has already proven himself with distinction.

One need only assemble a team of solid specialists to manage the administration and finances.

The great additional value that he possesses is his ability to create trust. That is the most important sort of capital a leader can have. People must believe in you. They must believe that you actually earn everything you have day by day, moment by moment.

Guardiola for president?

Why not? Many already had the impression during certain phases of the season that Pep was the president. During the summer break and President Laporta's return to the limelight, there were many comments expressing longing for the coach's return so that he might bring his wisdom to FC Barcelona, an institution so susceptible to emotion.

Will the institution and its periphery someday demonstrate the necessary maturity for this?

> *The leader who has the confidence of the people who depend on him possesses the greatest of all treasures.*

'YES WE PEP!'

One of the banners that could be seen most often in celebrating the first triple held the slogan 'Yes we Pep!' derived from the well-known 'Yes we can!' slogan made so popular by US president Barack Obama.

There is no doubt that the Catalan coach's fame has made him an idol of all Barça fans. But forever and always?

A top Catalan finance official told me the following once during a longer conversation:

'Let's not deceive ourselves. Guardiola will still have to pay his dues. Jealousy is the worst fault of the Catalans. Jealousy and self-loathing. We would give an eye if our neighbour were to lose two.'

It was a very candid discussion on the anthropological aspects of Catalan society where self-destructive tendencies are commonly observed.

From a historical viewpoint, Catalan writer Josep Pla already showed us this horrible quality of Catalonia. It bears profound individuality and generates jealousy.

Here we are dealing with a sufficiently researched and well-known sceptical alternative to the wave of euphoria created by FC Barcelona's sporting successes.

With this book I am in no way seeking to fuel this euphoria or wallow excessively in the latest achievements on the pitch. In my view, all types of euphoria are destructive as they warp one's sense of reality.

These are exactly the social values that give you the capacity to hold on to that sense of reality that is so important.

A hard-working and unselfish person does not allow himself to become so easily caught up in euphoria, as he knows how much effort it takes to earn success.

You do not have to convince a team player of the emotional benefits of joint effort. This can be seen in the fact that it is sensible to stay with the others and not stick one's head up even in the greatest hour of success.

You do not have to convince a grateful person of the beauty of their country, the importance of defending their cultural legacy or the significance of their roots.

You do not have to explain to a humble person that human history is also based on times of great violence and collective suffering. When a person has both feet solidly on the ground, he or she knows this already. They have suffered, have learned their lesson and have strove for understanding and intellect in order to lead a happy life.

This book is a clear acknowledgement of the values that made possible a wonderful sequence of athletic triumphs. Seven titles should be enough to convince us that intelligent efforts also bear fruit.

That leaders with distinct values also celebrate success.

That leaders with healthy common sense are capable of developing highly successful teams.

That it is worth the effort of following Pep Guardiola's example.

> *A leader whose actions are based on strong values possesses a sense of reality that allows him to come one step closer to success.*

THE ART OF LITTLE BIG DETAILS

A person with a predilection for details must be sensitive and a keen observer.

Pep carries both of these characteristics. In his public appearances, he demonstrates precision, *transparency* and a great deal of loyalty, which could also be described altogether as a human quality.

The modern media have circulated several examples of this:

Guardiola had just been appointed coach of Barça's first team when he purchased a plasma television out of his own pocket in order to be able to better track plays and draw appropriate conclusions.

When Juan Carlos Unzué's father passed away, Guardiola instructed the entire team to attend the funeral. That took place on 2 September 2008.

In doing this, he wanted to promote group cohesion through a sympathetic gesture in an especially difficult moment for an individual player. Some believed this measure was exaggerated and excessive and that it went too far. However, this very action became part of the foundation for good things to come.

In May of 2008, just before the birth of his daughter Valentina, Guardiola visited player Gabriel Milito to give him encouragement after the latter had suffered a serious injury causing him to take a year-and-a-half break from the game. (Milito returned to the pitch at the start of the 2010 season following his recovery.)

Before Guardiola's arrival, the team's evening meals were paid for with money from fines paid by players, but that changed. When Guardiola took over as coach, fine revenues were redirected to charitable purposes. It made little sense for money from fines to be used in part to reward wrongdoers.

The first organisation to receive a donation was the Sant Joan de Déu Foundation dedicated to researching Rett syndrome in children.

The Audi automobile company provides the team's players and the coach a new car every year, but this benefit is not extended to the rest of the training staff. Guardiola decided to do without his car so as to not place himself above the other members of his staff.

Thierry Henry's weak form in his first season caused Guardiola to invite him to dinner. Henry seemed transformed the next day in Barça's game against Valencia and scored three goals (a hat-trick). Henry had trouble gathering momentum in the following season and had to spend many games on the bench. His career with the Catalan team was approaching its end.

Cristóbal was a fan of limited financial means who often supported the players at the Miniestadi (the playing venue of Barcelona's reserve team). One day, Guardiola invited him to eat with the team. It must have been an unforgettable experience for Cristóbal who passed away shortly thereafter.

It is said that physical therapist Àngel Mur was left without a ticket to the Champions League final in Rome and that Pep intervened to get him into the game.

Guardiola treated the entire team to dinner at the best fish restaurant in A Coruña after Barça defeated Deportivo La Coruña in 2009.

'You are the best.' This dedication stood over a large photograph that he gave to his training staff after winning the triple.

When Albert Puig, trainer of the very youngest FC Barcelona players, presented his book dedicated to the young talents of La Masía titled *La força d'una il·lusió (The Power of a Dream)*, Pep participated in the event because he valued his colleague's work. Albert Puig, a great admirer of Pep, was deeply moved.

When Barcelona fell out of the running for the Spanish Cup in 2010 after a loss to Sevilla, Albert Puig said to Pep, *'Now that you've had your first loss, welcome to the coaches club.'*

After the victory in the FIFA World Club Championship in Abu Dhabi, Pep broke out in tears. The television cameras recorded several seconds of this and in doing so captured one of the most moving scenes in the Barcelona football history.

On 7 January 2010, Pep Guardiola and his two children visited Éric, a 12 year old at Vall d'Hebron Childrens Hospital.

'When you are out of here, you are going to train with us,' Guardiola promised him.

Éric passed away a few weeks later. Guardiola's caring words must have been a comfort to him.

I would like to add two stories that I heard.

Peps friends say that it is a special experience to go golfing with him. After the round, when the group is doing other things, Pep goes off to the side and doggedly repeats the strokes that he missed earlier to find out how to improve them. This is typical for him.

After the end of Pep's second season, a distinguished former FC Barcelona board member, who had secretly supported Pep to the best of his ability, received a photo of the coach at his office in the Ensanche district with the words *'I value you most of all!'*

LA MASÍA: A CHILD CARE CENTER FOR CHILD PRODIGIES

La Masía is one of the most wonderful things that FC Barcelona has. The youth academy was founded 30 years ago and has become a veritable breeding ground for outstanding players. Pep Guardiola was no exception either and first entered the academy at age 13.

An impressive generation of young talents has grown up there. FC Barcelona's first squad has profited from this above all. Of the multitude of great talent the academy has produced, several should be given special mention, such as Messi, Xavi and Iniesta. All three of these players have come to be considered some of the world's best.

That is a key to success: the unquestioning assumption of risk in promoting great talents. Pep Guardiola has especially distinguished himself in this regard as he as always promoted players from the youth academy. Pedro Rodríguez from Tenerife, the great discovery of 2010, is a good example of this. Guardiola has ensured that home-grown players are always in the majority on the Catalan team roster. The great dream of the blue-red fans has done more than come true, but Guardiola also understands how to harmoniously introduce foreign talents into the team. *Chapeau*. It is one of the young Catalan coach's greatest accomplishments.

Barcelona currently has three players from La Masía who are among the top five in the world: the aforementioned Xavi, Iniest and Messi—from Argentina who came to Barcelona in his tender years and was cared for by the blue-red institution. In 2009, Messi was selected as the best player in the world. A great success.

This is a perfect example of the fruit reaped from consistent and planned work with the next generation. It proves that when we undertake to organise things in Barcelona, we understand very well what we have to do. The results are players who set the global standard and export the prestige of the Barcelona brand around the world through their playing style and sense of sportsmanship.

Some of Messi's goals have evoked the applause of opposing fans. It is also not unusual for Xavi (2009 best European footballer of the year) and Iniesta to be seen off with applause when they leave the pitch at away games. This is the culture of recognising outstanding football. It is the fruit of a system that is equally aligned from the ground up. In actuality, all of Barcelona's youth teams cultivate the same playing style as the club's first team.

That is why great talents assimilate into the hierarchy in a very natural manner. Difficulties with adaptation are only minimal. The talent engine is running on all cylinders, and Pep Guardiola will ensure that that it remains that way by giving young players the chance to prove themselves. There are great talents who dream of playing in the first team squad someday just as he did.

The significance of this approach cannot be overestimated. Feeling like part of the whole develops in an entirely natural fashion. Giving young players a chance has also contributed to the creation of players such as Piqué, Valdés and Sergio Busquets.

Pep promotes self-reliance and personal appreciation and uses resources from within the club without closing the door to outside talents.

The management of FC Barcelona's talented next generation deserves a special word of praise for their achievements in recent years. Having said that, there is very little to criticise. One point of criticism would be the fact that the team failed to hang on to Barça youth-academy-trained Cesc Fàbregas who signed with Arsenal. He is a player who was given highest priority under president Sandro Rosell's leadership and ultimately returned to Barcelona in the summer of 2011.

THE 'WITH' CONCEPT—MAXIMUM MOTIVATION

How does one motivate people? That is the key question asked by all managers. Self-motivation is a sort of nirvana in the working world, but it is also a condition very difficult to achieve. All of us (including those who are sources of motivation) need someone to give us an extra boost of motivation from time to time.

Motivation is like the fuel that allows a car to drive. If a car runs out of petrol, it stays put.

This is why many motivational initiatives fall flat. They lack sustainability. Their developers lose sight of the flightiness of human nature. Motivation must be nurtured on a regular basis just as we have to put petrol in our car from time to time.

Provided that the members of a team have the right amount of talent, the best path to success is through creating a climate of motivation and dedication.

I have had the opportunity to visit the Massachusetts Institute of Technology (MIT) near Boston many times. Along with Harvard University, which is not far away, it is the world's largest think tank in terms of innovations in technology and the arts.

What especially catches my eye about these institutions is the passion with which the people there dedicate themselves to the task at hand and their commitment to their own work.

It goes without saying that certain consideration must be given for the intelligence and outstanding education of the students, professors and researchers there although they are actually taken for granted. However, the most important key to success is devotion to work and constantly striving for excellent performance.

Working hours are secondary in this regard. Peoples' minds are primarily focused on achieving goals. The system provides an infrastructure for this, which promotes experimentation and does not punish failure. Many buildings are truly open 24 hours a day. Proper identification is all that's required to enter at night.

That is something that MIT deputy finance director Israel Ruiz, a native of Barcelona, told me in a conversation in his office. He is a 'culé,' meaning a fervent supporter of FC Barcelona. (He showed me his large writing pen bearing the club's crest used for signing all contracts.)

The success of MIT can be explained by two factors: the talent of individuals and the system's capacity to promote them. The fact that the best professors teach there in turn attracts the best students who, for their part, strive to achieve optimum results.

Thus, a system designed for outstanding performance is created automatically. Israel Ruiz describes the underlying formula as follows: outstanding performance promotes a meritocracy (the best on top), which favours learning by doing, which favours inventive capabilities. When one

learns by doing, it becomes appropriate and even necessary to enter unknown territory. When implemented, this system creates motivation. Motivation influences people's lives, meaning it causes outcomes favouring a spiral of excellent performance. In this way, each factor affects all of the remaining factors in a positive manner.

According to Israel Ruiz, Barcelona's youth academy's mode of operation is like that of MIT. Only the best are accepted to La Masía, and, of those selected, only a minority make it to the first squad, though this number has increased in size during Guardiola's tenure.

There is no doubt that the act of accumulating talented individuals in one place creates more of the same. When a certain environment is created, those who belong there will quite naturally accept certain guiding principles for improvement, and this results in constantly increasing standards. It is a train that never stops and always travels faster and faster.

A solid foundation is necessary to achieve this, but time also plays an important role. The fruit is only ready to harvest after a certain amount of time has passed. Structural improvements can obviously shorten the length of some processes, but consideration must always be given for the time required for natural maturation.

It is a sort of logic that demands growth. A core is created to guarantee exceptional performance, and that core assures the availability of new resources for further expansion. New fields are created that continue to grow as long as performance remains at the same high level.

I asked Israel Ruiz if La Masía could also become an elite coach training centre and if Guardiola could be the one to launch such an initiative.

He replied that we would have to see whether Guardiola is capable of communicating his unique method. There are people who can do things very well but are incapable of communicating how they do it to others.

My personal impression is that Guardiola would be fully capable of this because he has the great ability to place himself in the position of others. Furthermore, he is very generous. This is another fundamental prerequisite for communicating the key factors of one's own success.

The bottom line is that talent requires talent in order to grow and reproduce. For full advantage to be taken of the available human potential, this talent must first and foremost be reflected in the organisational structure of the habitat where it is meant to develop and in the methodology used. One must offer the players an environment that guarantees constant development and personal satisfaction for them to be able to exploit their abilities and do so on a constant basis.

I have often asked myself why in Catalonia and in Spain we are not capable of creating such conditions, or at least, why it is so difficult for us. We have no lack of talent. We have a privileged geographic location, a rich history and great cultural diversity. What are we missing then?

It is likely an issue of fundamental attitudes and the underlying culture. It is difficult for us to highlight all of our abilities through teamwork. We lack an understanding of collective achievement and leaders with both comprehensive abilities and an eye for the whole picture who give meticulous consideration to every detail.

In moments such as these, when I reach these conclusions and take a look at Guardiola's career, I notice that Catalonia has indeed overcome its traditional limitations. Pep managed to weld together a team, bring out the best in every player and staff member and set an exceptional example in doing so.

VALUES AND

MORE VALUES

VALUES AND
MORE VALUES ▪ ▪ ▪

One of the Spanish thinkers that knows so much about values is philosopher and theologian Francesc Torralba. He makes this clear in his remarkable work titled *Francesc Torralba (100 Values for Life)*. Torralba is also an avid athlete with blue-red blood flowing in his veins.

In January of 2010, I had the opportunity to speak with him on my book programme called *Les bones obres on Ràdio Estel* and could not help asking him a few questions about Pep Guardiola.

A few days later, I published the most significant portions of his comments in the *Catalunya Cristiana* newspaper under the title 'Guardiola as a Paradigm of an Outstanding Leadership Style.'

The young FC Barcelona coach was mentioned in the following portions of the interview:

Miguel Angel Violán: *The sports world demands heroic feats. What is your view of FC Barcelona's latest victories and especially of Pep Guardiola?*

Francesc Torralba: *Every leader must have values. Those who coach teams are successful if they impart certain values: wisdom, confidence and humility. I believe that these are the keys to Barça's success today.*

MAV: *Which values does Pep Guardiola demonstrate as a leader?*

FT: *He is prepared for self-sacrifice, intelligent, tough, discrete, elegant, capable of welding a team together, he knows how to lose but how to win as well...Those are values that can be imparted to others only with great difficulty, especially if one is dealing with a group of pronounced individualists. Guardiola is a paradigm of this. When values become flesh and blood, societies blossom.*

MAV: *Can Guardiola's values be applied to other areas as well?*

FT: *I believe so. For example: in schools, factories or companies. They are values that one must have at the forefront.*

GUARDIOLA'S VALUES CATALOGUE

With my interview of Francesc Torralba in mind, I looked deeper into the world of values and Torralba's standardisation of them.

Following is a list of 100 values that the philosopher and theologian presents in his book. It is difficult to find a value or characteristic that Pep Guardiola does not possess. Readers can verify this using the following list:

1. Alterity
2. Friendship
3. Education
4. Hospitality
5. Trust
6. Ability to dialogue
7. Brotherliness
8. Honour
9. Forgiveness
10. Faithfulness
11. Acceptance
12. Coherence
13. Dedication
14. Meditation/Reflection
15. Presence/Physicality
16. Elegance
17. Flexibility
18. Altruism
19. Cheerfulness
20. Supportiveness

21. Benevolence

22. Ecological awareness

23. Calmness

24. Eruditeness

25. Thrift

26. Passivity

27. Gratitude

28. Cosmic solidarity

29. Simplicity

30. Sustainability

31. Politeness

32. Gentleness

33. Respect

34. Sympathy

35. Tact

36. Cordiality

37. Discretion

38. Generosity

39. Sensitivity

40. Sobriety

41. Tranquillity

42. Beauty

43. Concentration

44. Enthusiasm

45. Serenity

46. Uniqueness

47. Solitariness

48. Composure

49. Understanding

50. Restiveness

51. Strength

52. Humility

53. Sense for secrecy

54. Patience

55. Ability to listen

56. Tenacity

57. Compassion

58. Abstinence

59. Veracity

60. Resilience

61. Spontaneity

62. Fun

63. Humour

64. Playfulness

65. Shrewdness

66. Curiosity

67. Respectability

68. Tolerance

69. Sincerity

70. Good conversationalist

71. Diligence

72. Honesty

73. Imagination

74. Competitiveness

75. Cleverness

76. Punctuality

77. Agility

78. Strictness

79. Efficiency

80. Availability

81. Memory

82. Seriousness

83. Sense of responsibility

84. Equality

85. Innocence

86. Liberty

87. Epikeia
(moral behaviour)

88. Filial love
(for one's parents)

89. Rationality

90. Sufferance

91. Credulity

92. Creativity

93. Courageousness

94. Ability to criticise

95. Stamina

96. Faith

97. Magnanimity

98. Peacefulness

99. Righteousness

100. Hope

GUARDIOLA AND POLITICAL INTELLIGENCE

We often speak about how important it is for organisations to have a high level of emotional intelligence. This well-known term was coined by North American journalist and psychologist David Goleman. It is the requirement that those in leadership, just like all types of professionals, be capable of controlling their emotions and empathising with others. Without this attribute, there can be no harmonious relations within an organisation.

However, we do not speak as often about another type of intelligence that is just as important. We can call it *political intelligence*. Simply put, it is the ability to use power relationships to one's advantage.

Organisations are structures that either feature power relationships or have developed from them. Some give instructions, and others carry them out. There are also those who more or less do both. These power relationships build on the interests at play, and the capacity to act is limited by the ethical code of the organisation in question or by the protagonists.

In this regard, political instinct signifies the following:

- Interaction of existing forces
- Capturing the minds and loyalty of the employees, meaning those who are theoretically in one's charge
- The ability to analyse what the best decision is at all times to protect one's interests

■ The ability to form alliances with those with whom one wants to avoid conflict even if the other party is intent on causing such conflict (exactly what one wants to avoid)

■ The ability to assess and recognise those who might damage one's interests as well as those to whom one might turn for protection or for reparation of resulting damages

Pep Guardiola demonstrated great political intelligence in his relationship with FC Barcelona president Joan Laporta. Even if it was not easy for him, he was successful in this regard time and again. For example, he shielded the dressing room from the board of directors and the mass media, both of which were constantly on the lookout for the smallest indiscretions and the latest unpleasant details.

At the same time, Guardiola respected the institutional office of the president with a sense of humility but without any servility. When he was meant to be grateful, he was grateful. For example, his first statements upon winning his seventh title 4:0 against Real Valladolid at Camp Nou were words of appreciation for the years of selfless work on behalf of the club that he directed towards the outgoing president.

It is wonderful to see how Guardiola positioned himself as Barcelona's most valuable asset. His personal brand is consistent with the club's high standards and even superior to them in some aspects.

I was able to observe this during the seminars that I held on *The Guardiola Method* throughout Spain before this book was published. In April of 2010, I was in the city of Algeciras, a bulwark of Real Madrid and a bastion of typical Spanish values. No fewer than 15 participants explicitly stated their admiration for Guardiola during the question and answer session…and their rejection of Laporta.

How can two people born in the same country evoke such divergent sentiments?

Guardiola knew how to coexist with a controversial president who doubtlessly had good sense. When Laporta ended up on the ropes after a traumatic no-confidence vote, he decided to listen to those who recommended Guardiola as a means of bringing the blue-red ship back on course.

There are moments and decisions in the lives of both people and organisations that hold strategic significance. They are known as turning points in the U.S. They mark the beginning of a new course.

Laporta decided in favour of a winning option. History must give him credit for this service.

INSPIRING IMAGES AND SOUNDS

Music and images were constantly present during the first two years of Pep Guardiola's tenure as coach of the first team squad.

Beyond the young Catalan coach's cultural preferences, images and music have been considered extremely effective motivational and leadership tools for some time.

Who among us has not been captured when hearing a long forgotten melody reminiscent of a beautiful moment in the past? Who among us has not felt the power of a photograph immortalising a seemingly forgotten moment already partially lost from the archives of our memories?

These are trusted techniques in the fields of coaching and management consulting. They are consistent with the use of neurolinguistic programming and thought structuring to achieve better results as well as the techniques of relaxation and visualisation.

The images from the film *Gladiator* that Pep used to inspire his players before the final in Rome have become the mostly widely known. The film is well known and the moment he selected was historic: FC Barcelona's third Champions League title win.

Pep Guardiola discovered his passion for music long ago. Among other occasions, we saw him singing at the farewell concert for this friend Lluís Llach in Verges.

This was one of many occasions.

Pep has also applied the power of music with his players as a tool for strengthening their sensitivity. A footballer who understands what he represents and the framework in which he does so will run differently on the pitch. He will give it everything he has because he carries a feeling of indebtedness to others and a willingness to serve them.

When FC Barcelona won 4:0 against Valladolid in May of 2010 and clinched the Spanish title for a second time, Peps words were more than significant:

'We owed it to you.'

It was a declaration of a viewpoint that also expressed the ambition of a team dedicated to a high-performance sport. It was a demonstration for the most important stakeholders, the fans, that the team was at their service.

It was one of the most exceptional statements ever to be heard on a football pitch.

THE SPIRIT OF BILLY ELLIOT

Billy Elliot is one of the most beautiful films showing motivation and tenacity in overcoming obstacles. A British miner's son growing up in a world of strikes and without a mother, Billy's desire is to devote himself to dancing. However, he is confronted with his father's resistance to this and the latter's view that dancing is something reserved for girls.

The film's impressive scenes are exemplary of the importance of persistence in achieving one's dreams.

One of the great moments of the film comes towards the end when Billy performs before a selected jury, which will decide whether he receives a coveted stipend. The jury asks the boy to dance.

The faces of the jury members change as they recognise Billy's talent. Their strict manner disappears, and they display the sort of delighted astonishment that one has when making a great discovery.

It is an unforgettable scene and worth watching 1,001 times for those who feel an artistic or related calling in life.

Billy's spirit reflects the determination to not give up on one's own dreams.

(If a pedagogue manages to impart this to his or her students, the doors to success open wide. Everything interlocks, and you move in the desired direction automatically just like on an assembly line.)

After Billy's performance, the jury asks him what he feels when he dances. The boy's words are an exact description of what humanistic psychologist Abraham Maslow called peak experiences. They are moments when there is neither a lack nor overabundance of anything. Everything is flowing. Invisibility. One feels like pure electricity. Time stands still. Life is perfect. The world is exactly the way it should be.

The highest (and richest) objective of a pedagogue is to make the learning process an accumulation of high points.

GUARDIOLA'S PRAETORIAN GUARD

One of the keys to Barcelona's great success is its first guard (of football players) whose members have their feet on the ground, are hard-workers and modest and are permeated with the values taught in the youth academy.

How else could a dressing room become such a successful melting pot of harmonised local and foreign talent that lacks significant conflicts and possesses the strong feeling of belonging that is seen in the players-circle ritual after warm-up each game?

Puyol, Xavi Hernàndez, Iniesta and even Messi have pedigree and are footballers who implement their coach's expectations, values and instructions with a great degree of efficiency. The coach is surrounded by veteran staff members. These are important people such as Tito Vilanova, a friend of Guardiola's from his La Masía days, and Paco Seirullo, a veritable institution in the field of sports medicine.

There is a solid backbone of players that prevent motivation from plummeting and players from breaking away from the team to pursue the celebrity lifestyle. They keep team members from feeling like lost sheep as happened with Ronaldinho three years ago.

One has only to observe the presence of these home-grown players to understand the team's behaviour. They represent the unequivocal will to win as well as their own identity: They belong to Barça.

To a large extent, Barcelona's triumphs in recent years can be traced back to this internal lobby, this Praetorian Guard that internalises, understands and implements the coach's instructions.

On the other hand, there are also mentor relationships among the players. For example, Milito exerts a positive influence on Messi, for whom he is a very important pillar of emotional support. Henry, for his part, is something of a brother to the young Bojan.

These are the interpersonal relationships that weld the group together and provide the emotional stability required among a profession characterised by imbalances, setbacks, press besiegement and constant temptations of vanity.

HOW LLUÍS BASSAT MADE HIMSELF HEARD ON CATALUNYA RÀDIO

'He must be well prepared.'

That is what the Catalunya Ràdio staff members on duty must have thought when they saw publicist Lluís Bassat running to the radio studio after midnight sometime in the first half of 2010. He was there to respond to the commentaries that had been made about him during journalist Pere Escobar's expert round table discussion.

Bassat was on the way home (he lived close to the radio station on the corner of Diagonal and Beethoven Street) when he heard some comments on the radio questioning whether he understood anything about football. When passing by, Bassat saw an open parking space in front of the radio station and immediately parked his car, ran up to the building and asked to be let on the air live.

A surprised Escobar turned on a microphone and gave Bassat the floor.

'I do not know whether I understand a little or a lot about football. However, I do know something about people.'

Lluís Bassat had run for the presidency of FC Barcelona (which he incidentally lost), and his candidate for the club's athletic management had been Pep Guardiola. At that time, Joan Laporta accused Bassat of lacking football knowledge and Guardiola of wanting for experience.

Joan Laporta would rely on this very same Pep Guardiola years later after narrowly escaping removal from office due to a no-confidence vote.

Lluís Bassat had the opportunity of getting to know Guardiola during a long conversation in Italy years before. They had spoken with one another from noon until six in the evening.

'He actually did everything that he told me he was going to do then, and he has been greatly successful,' revealed Lluís Bassat who had predicted a great future for the FC Barcelona coach at the end of his career in coaching.

When we asked him about this, he replied,

'He could be an outstanding sports director, an outstanding vice president and even an outstanding president of FC Barcelona.' Those were the words of Bassat who admitted that he and Guardiola share several character traits, including stubbornness and excessive sensitivity.

Bassat had put his cards on Guardiola. Even at that time, he saw in Guardiola many of the virtues that others would not notice until much later. Even Joan Laporta demonstrated presence of mind and courage and ultimately decided in favour of the young coach who had never been responsible for a team in either the first or second Liga.

'I do know something about people.' This succinct phase spoken by Lluís Bassat reveals a characteristic trait of his professional career. He possesses the ability to surround himself with talented people and always adheres to the guidelines he establishes for himself.

HOW MUST MODERN LEADERS BE?

Harvard Business School (HBS) is considered one of the best economics universities in the world. It may also be the most prestigious, and that is why it sets the standard. HBS is renowned for its pragmatic methodology and the multitude of gurus that speak in its lecture halls. The majority of these experts are the *crème de la crème* of global executive board members.

The university appointed Indian professor Nitin Nohria, a proven specialist in the field of leadership among other things, as its dean to take over the institution in a time of crisis in May of 2010. The society was in particular need of leadership and was characterised by Obama as a reference for life in the U.S.

Nohria had published the *Handbook of Leadership* together with fellow Harvard Business School professor Rakesh Kurana. It was a modern compendium of viewpoints by important representatives of the academic world on leadership following a certain decline of this topic as a field of study because it is impossible to reliably quantify leadership qualities.

We are currently experiencing a reassessment of this subject, giving it an increasing level of importance. This is why the number of academic works on this theme will continue to grow in coming years.

It was the same Harvard Business School that organised the Centennial Colloquium on the occasion of its 100th anniversary two years ago, using both standard and new technologies (e.g., Twitter and other social networks) to accept contributions from around the globe throughout 2009 and 2010.

The big question is: How must new leaders be in these highly complex times of rapid change?

This topic goes back in the academic world to a time when there was still no light at the end of the tunnel. (Harvard University, the world's most wealthy university, lost one third of its assets as a result of the global financial crisis. Nonetheless, these assets are still greater than the gross domestic product of many of the world's countries.)

There were renewed debates about how trust is gained, how to lead the way by setting a good example and how to ensure total dedication to the cause. The question was how to weld people together and inspire them all.

It is ultimately a conversation about how one uses the support of others to pull chestnuts out of a fire.

One of the considerations that we have to make is associated with the significant impact Guardiola's two winning years had on the general spiritual condition. In a time of crisis in which consumption is on the rise and faith in tomorrow is on the decline, the Catalan team's good performance provided an important balancing factor, a measure of joy and proof that every effort is worthwhile. They are what enable us to achieve any goal imaginable.

In the same way, there are also a number of values associated with personal effort that should not be left out.

This is Pep Guardiola's important lesson.

(A side story: When a close staff member had to give a presentation on the topic of what makes a leader, he asked Guardiola this very question. Pep scratched his head for a few seconds and replied, *'I don't have the foggiest idea.'*)

LAST BUT NOT LEAST:

THE EIGHTH TITLE

LAST BUT NOT LEAST:
THE EIGHTH TITLE ■ ■ ■

FC Barcelona players Pedro Rodríguez and Víctor Valdés were on the Spanish national team for the first time at the 2010 World Cup in South Africa. Valdés had never been considered for the team up to that point.

In view of the impressive number of blue-red players in the Spanish line-up, many fans (some with mixed feelings) saw the World Cup as an opportunity to win Barça's eighth title. Carles Puyol's header goal off of Xavi's perfectly executed pass against Germany launched the team into the final against the Netherlands, and Andrés Iniesta's outstanding goal in the final minutes of overtime of that game produced a triumph for Spain. It was a reward well-earned for national coach Vicente del Bosque. At the same time, it was an open secret that Spain had won the championship with Guardiola's model.

However, Guardiola had actually already won his eighth title before that. In actuality, it was his very first title, a victory that was not recorded as such in the official statistics. I am speaking of when Barça B rose from the third to the second league. This transition was the work of a certain Guardiola who was debuting as the coach of FC Barcelona's second team.

Those close to Pep say that this title was the most important of all to him, as he had to work the hardest for it. Moreover, it opened doors for his successes to come.

Things possess a value directly related to the effort invested in them. Winning a multitude of titles in the past few years would not have been possible with the self-sacrificing work of many previous generations at Barcelona. They were the ones who ultimately created the conditions for the seeds of success to sprout and blossom.

This generation must be reminded of this above all, as they only know Barça as being a winning team. They know Barça's current *Belle Époque* and view victory as the most natural thing in the world.

New times with different challenges will come. Nothing is guaranteed. Only one thing will remain constant: Values and attitudes determine the final results.

Leaders with common sense know this, and that is why they are exceptionally successful.

Boston, 31 May 2010

BOOKS & OTHER

RESOURCES

BOOKS &
OTHER RESOURCES ■ ■ ■

BOOKS

I am a person who loves to make book recommendations. This has come to apply to all types of cultural resources as well. After all, I have been dedicated to giving reading suggestions on *Ràdio Estel* for 16 years.

There are a handful of books and other resources that I suggest in order to expand one's knowledge of Pep Guardiola and his football environment. Following are my favourite books selected from those that I know. This list makes no claims whatsoever at being comprehensive. It is simply my small selection.

Jaume Collell, Pep Guardiola: De Santpedor al banquillo del Barça (Pep Guardiola: From Santpedor to the Coach's Bench at Barça). Published by Península. A book that came out at the right time as it was published during Guardiola's first season. It provides an engaging description of Pep's origins, stories from his life and the people who have influenced him. Many later works reference this book and quote it from time to time. It's a good read.

Josep Guardiola, La meva gent, el meu futbol (My People, My Football), with a foreword by Pep's friend, David Trueba, and written in cooperation with journalists Miguel Rico and Luis Martín. Published in the collection Sport. I have a copy from 2001, and it goes without saying that it has come to have exceptional value. The book describes Pep's ability to adopt and coalesce the legacy and lessons of the many people he has come in contact with thus far in his life.

Ferran Soriano, La pelota no entra por azar (The Ball Doesn't Go In By Chance). Published by Leqtor. FC Barcelona attracted the interest of the academic world two years ago. This is a book of substance with a clear thesis. It has the feeling of a platform designed to present a future candidate for the club's presidency that was ultimately not used. The airline Spanair (an entrepreneurial project that failed in 2011) bears the 'blame' for this.

Josep Riera Font, Escoltant Guardiola: El pensament futbolístic i vital de l'entrenador del Barça en 150 frases (Listen to Guardiola: The Thoughts of Barça's Coach on Football and Life in 150 Phrases). Published by Cossetània Edicions. It is a compendium of Font's explanations helping to understand Guardiola's dialectics and also a collection of opinions of exceptional representatives of the game of football.

Albert Puig, La fuerza de un sueño (The Power of a Dream). Published by Plataforma Editorial. How is the character of future stars formed at La Masía? That is what the coach of the youngest Barcelona players describes in this book. He is a kind man with a clear sense of sportsmanship. He is one of those who emphasise the importance of role models.

Àlex Santos Fernàndez, L'entorn. El circ mediàtic del Barça (The Environment. The Media Circus of Barça). Published by Cossetània Edicions. This book is the final work in a trilogy on the club and was written by an experienced journalist who is still just as happy as ever to be working in this field.

Agustí Montal, Memòries d'un president blaugrana en temps difícils (Memories of a Barcelona President in Difficult Times). Published by Proa. The testimony of an important man in contemporary Barça history. I interviewed him on Ràdio Estel. In the summer of 1977, I became acquainted with his daughter (since passed away) flying San Francisco–Los Angeles–Madrid–Barcelona. I told him about this when the microphones were off, and we were both very moved.

Juan Carlos Cubeiro and Leonor Gallardo, Liderazgo Guardiola: des- cubre los secretos de su éxito (Guardiola the Leader: Discover the Secret of His Success). Published by Alienta Editorial. This is a compendium of texts about Guardiola accompanied by the authors' comments and knowledge of leadership and sports management. It contains an impressive epilogue by former FC Barcelona board member Gabriel Masfurroll in which he coins the term blue-red DNA. The foreword was written by Susanna Griso, a Catalan journalist, with what is probably the greatest inner beauty in existence. The same authors subsequently wrote the books Mourinho versus Guardiola (Mourinho versus Guardiola) and Los Mosqueteros de Guardiola (Guardiola's Musketeers).

Nitin Nohria und Rakesh Khurana, The Handbook of Leadership: Theory and Practice. Published by Harvard University Press in May of 2010. This work is ideal for odd people like me who study leadership. This book explains the state of the art in regards to leadership theory and summarises the opinions of various renowned experts from around the globe. Nitin Nohria was the co-ordinator of this comprehensive work. A scientist and leadership expert born in Bombay, Nohria was appointed dean of Harvard Business School in July of 2010. It took just three hours for him to respond to my email when I informed him of the publishing of The Guardiola Method. (Many academicians in Spain could learn something from his example.)

Lecture Series Valors útils per a Catalunya del futur (Useful Values for the Catalonia of the Future). Held in Barcelona in the fall of 2008 with support from the Lluís Carulla Foundation and the Centre d'Estudis Jordi Pujol.

SPORTS REPORTING

Articles by Ramon Besa in the *El País* daily newspaper prove very useful in terms of understanding Guardiola's universe and are written from the viewpoint of a stern and balanced journalist who admires him while maintaining the distance indispensable in sports reporting.

Thank you Ramon and congratulations on receiving the Premio Internacional de Periodismo Manuel Vázquez Montalbán.

I have a very critical view of sports reporting. However, I also believe that there are many journalists who do outstanding work and earn every recognition they receive.

They also deserve support in light of the lamentable fact that there are media corporations that do not exactly make their job any easier. It should be the other way around.

I can only recommend Joan Golobart's analytical articles in *La Vanguardia*. They communicate the tactical, psychological and social subtleties of football in a thoughtful and balanced manner. I am an avid reader of his articles.

I also follow the analyses of journalist Martí Perarnau with interest. He presents a series of interesting notions about La Masía as a talent factory in his book titled *El camí dels campions (The Way of Champions)* published by Columna Edicions.

For those who enjoy comprehensive viewpoints of things and have a passionate interest in music, the arts and quantum physics, it might be worthwhile glancing through a book titled *El Barça by Sandro Modeo,* published by Ediciones Alfabia.

Fans of technical and tactical issues of the Barça squad under Pep's leadership should visit the blog called *Paradigma Guardiola (The Guardiola Paradigm)* maintained by Matías Manna from Argentina: *http:// paradigmaguardiola. blogspot.com.es/*

Also of interest on the subject, the book *Fórmula Barça (The Barça Formula)* by Catalunya Ràdio journalist and confirmed analyst Ricard Torquemada is essential to understanding Barça's development in recent years. Published by Cossetània Edicions.

The round table discussions held under the title *Tu diràs* on RAC1 were a lot of fun for me. I listen to them frequently online in the farthest corners of the world and at the most unimaginable times of day. What I like most is the talent of moderator Joan Maria Pou and, currently, that of Dani Senabre. As for the participants of these discussions, all viewpoints are represented but that is also the appeal of this programme. I personally had the opportunity of participating not long ago.

I would also like to take this opportunity to remember the mythical sports reporters of the 1970s, especially Miguel Angel Valdivieso who awoke my interest in the language of sports. I especially recall his somewhat odd wording (typical for that time) in reading out things, such as the inevitable greeting to the very pleasant 'members of the national organisation for the blind.'

TELEVISION

In March of 2011, *Millennium* on TV3 dedicated an entire programme to the topic of 'Leaders.' It was a pleasure to be able to speak with José Antonio Marina, one of my favourite authors, about the Guardiola method. It was also fun to draw public attention to how important it is for economics universities to return to true values and not deal with shooting off fireworks.

http://www.tv3.cat/videos/3436250/Ser-liders

Another interview with me can be seen on Channel 9 in Tarragona. During this programme, I assert that Mourinho only wants to win while Pep aims to persuade. As was once written in a local newspaper, 'Pep represents a productive economy' while 'Mourinho represents speculation.'

http://www.youtube.com/watch?v=pof1m7JJiNc

I also participated in a colloquium on the Guardiola method in the Divendres programme on TV3:

http://www.youtube.com/watch?v=WS05fhDxhP0

We held an event with the provocative title *Guardiola, l'heroi perfecte? (Guardiola, the Perfect Hero?)* in the Excellence bookstore in Barcelona. It took place on a Saturday morning, the very same super successful 21 May 2011, the day of the Champions League final against Manchester United at Wembley Stadium. It was extremely interesting. It also led to a new project of mine—a work still in progress: an effort to launch a discussion forum titled *Guardiolistes sense Fronteres (Guardiola Fans Without Limits),* a reference to the limits of knowledge on the multifaceted profile of his personality.

Moderated by Hortènsia Galí, the colloquium was quite lively. Participants included psychologist Antoni Bolinches, author Lluís Racionero, journalist Joan Armengol, author Míriam Subirana, Dr. Eduard Estivill, Dr. Daniel Brotons, music journalist Jordi Bianciotto, actor Bernat Quintana, Banco de Sabadell marketing director Elisabet Valls, author Carlos Alonso and two representatives of the Excellence bookstore, Víctor Tébar (creative lab director) and Félix Velasco (business after work).

Several pictures of the event can be viewed here:

http://www.youtube.com/watch?v=fWHericsTM4

And if you want to have a little fun, I can only recommend you watch Toni Soler's comedy programme *Cracròvia.* Humour and caricatures sometimes reveal the truth better than any other type of classical journalism.

Many clips of this programme can be found at: www.youtube.com. I am not ashamed to admit that we take great pleasure in watching this programme at home.

In conclusion, I would also like to mention Carles Folguera, director of La Masía, and Josep Maria Prat, FC Barcelona cultural advisor. Both of these individuals sharpened my awareness of the value of education and culture for Barca in the 21st century during my conversations with them. I now understand that we are dealing with a highly respected worldwide brand rising at meteoric speed.

You can follow my commentaries on the current situation with FC Barcelona on my blog called Esto es lo que hay (This Is What's Happening). I have been using this as a forum to report all sorts of experiences, including my own work (which started out innocently enough) in guardiology.

http://blogs.periodistadigital.com/estoesloquehay.php

ER
B
O

to live
s MAR
h cheap

ut hav
ried abou
en you ma

r and have
d study visi
urther infor

di

che

FOUR

COMMENTARIES

FOUR
COMMENTARIES ■ ■ ■

Antoni Bolinches, psychologist: 'The Guardiola Method or Guardiola as a Method?'

Daniel Brotons, MD: 'Challenge to Play With Insight'

Xarli Diego, journalist: 'Miguel Angel, How Did You Even Do That?'

Felipe Cuesta, solicitor: 'Love and Prayers: The 5th Project'

THE GUARDIOLA METHOD OR
GUARDIOLA AS A METHOD

by Antoni Bolinches, clinical psychologist, author, and creator of vital therapy

I am not a football expert. My life priorities do not include identifying myself with some team to share in its victories and defeats. Nonetheless, I know a lot about the effects of success on people.

It is from this standpoint that I will make my contribution to this interesting book written by my good friend and outstanding author, Miguel Angel Violán. I have been holding interesting discussions on psychosocial topics for many years now in various Catalunya Ràdio programmes including the legendary El suplement with Xavier Solà, which received an Ondas Award in 2005.

In this regard, and also with respect to the title of the book, the first question that I ask myself is whether Guardiola has a method or whether Guardiola himself is a method.

For you to understand where I'm coming from, I would like to say that I was one of the first to introduce Rogers Therapy in Spain before I developed my own therapeutic procedure. Rogers Therapy was based on the belief that people are capable of improving themselves and solving their problems when they believe in their own capabilities and develop their skills.

For the topic of discussion here, Pep Guardiola's success as a football coach, I believe the phenomenon can be explained by referring to Carl R. Rogers. What he said was, 'Behaviour is the method.'

When I applied this to our topic of interest and consider the speech and behaviour of this coach who rose so swiftly to fame, I arrive at the conclusion that he is an intuitive user of the Rogers method even if he is unaware of it. The justification: He knew how to fulfil the three conditions in his team specified in Rogers Therapy for fostering success in all human activity dependent on collaboration and group harmony among people for success.

The first condition is that each member of the group be confident in his or her abilities.

The second is to discover the ideal environment for the abilities of the individual members of the group.

The third requires that each party understand that personal performance is strengthened through recognising and accepting the performance of others.

Only the skilful handling of these three conditions can explain how a team consisting primarily of the same players as the year before could improve its game and success rate in the well-known and spectacular way it did in 2009 and the following two years.

So when I attempt to analyse the success of the Guardiola method using my skill set, I arrive at the conclusion that the answer lies in the person of the coach.

In this regard, we can assume that Pep's success is the natural consequence of implicit application of the fundamental requirements of personal development therapies. These therapies represent the thesis that the success of a treatment method is above all dependent on the credibility of the person applying it and not on the technical procedures involved.

So when I analyse the objectives of FC Barcelona from the standpoint of group dynamics and leadership, I arrive at the conclusion that all of the conditions are fulfilled to establish that Guardiola does not have a method and that it is more likely that he is the method. His behaviour is characterised by authenticity and congruency, and he was capable of developing a relationship dynamic through learning by example.

This learning takes place as the players take on the coach's values. They use them as a guideline for their own behaviour because they accept them as a model. They use these values to further develop their own personality.

For this reason, I would like to repeat that Guardiola himself is the method. He knew how to inject his team with the values he possesses. The players recognise his authority in the field of football that he earned through his experience as an active player and his maturity.

However, there is a dark side to everything. From now on, Guardiola's problem will be to remain at the level of these successes. This will be difficult for him. When one is at the very top, the only place to go is down.

I would dare to claim that if the young and brilliant coach who so quickly rose to fame is capable of processing all of that, he could become a role model of the very best quality for those who understand that outstanding team performance is only possible when its leader is a recognised positive reference.

It is a matter of a person whose abilities are uncontested because they are based on his own competence and career to date.

For this reason, it should not be difficult for the current FC Barcelona coach to predict that much more success and recognition awaits him even if it remains to be seen how much of this will be attributed to him in the club where he has developed thus far. Another psychological principle that underlies all interpersonal relationships is that of saturation, and for this reason, the Guardiola cycle will someday come to an end.

When he was appointed coach of the first squad, I said publically on Josep Cunis' programme Els Matins (The Mornings) on TV3 that it would be good and sensible for both him and the club. I would now like to add to this that this co-operative effort should be maintained as long as possible and that its length should not affect the club's success.

Fortunately, there is now a book available to assess all of the psychosocial variables that make it possible to take mature and considered decisions, and I have the great pleasure of writing a commentary on this book. I have done this for four important reasons.

The first reason is that it is a useful book at the right time. The second reason is that it was written by a friend.

The third reason is that I receive the pleasure of expressing my opinion in this forum together with three individuals who are highly respected for both their professional and personal qualities: Dr Daniel Brotons, journalist and consultant Xarli Diego and solicitor Felipe Cuesta.

The fourth reason is as follows: Even though I established at the beginning that I understand nothing of football, it is still a great pleasure for me to express my views on a sociological phenomenon brought about by a player and coach of the same club where I once admired a magician with the ball named Ladislao Kubala as a child.

CHALLENGE TO PLAY WITH INSIGHT

by Daniel Brotons i Cuixart, physician and chairman of the Societat Catalana de Medicina de l'Esport

My profession requires that I occupy myself fully and without limitation with people who do sports. They do this as a hobby, because the doctor ordered it or because it is their profession.

It goes without saying that I work with all three groups, but it is also true that I have always felt especially drawn to high-performance sports.

By this I mean sports requiring hard training, discipline, a constant fight to overcome personal boundaries, endless self-sacrifice and many hours of hard work.

Many of these sports are scarcely media material and enjoy only limited acknowledgement by society.

It is likely for this reason that I have often had a very critical attitude towards football, as the 'social' rewards in professional football are in no way proportional to effort required. Whatever the reasons for this (media influence, fan expectations or a very singular environment), there has come to be a decreasing amount of beauty in this sport for us to admire as everything has become focused on a minimalistic objective: whether the ball goes in or not.

Pep Guardiola was appointed coach and swiftly earned the respect and admiration of not only the fans but also of society as a whole.

Guardiola never promised to win a title. He promised to be a team of which lovers of beautiful football could be proud.

I believe that Pep has succeeded in making it possible for the essential beauty of football to come to the fore once again. On the other hand, he has also created a group dynamic based on established rules of work and behaviour for which he has consistently led by setting a good example.

Guardiola understood how to exact perfect control over all of the factors that could lead to the team's destabilization: from injury at inopportune moments to excessive media pressure.

Moreover, he has surrounded himself with a highly professional staff of advisors who are constantly on top of what is happening.

Guardiola dedicated himself to constant correction of little details in terms of both interpersonal relations and technical issues. The sum of all this brought about great changes in the group he leads. His efforts have been crowned with capital success.

As doctors, we first listen to our patients and then examine their ailments, give a diagnosis and apply the most sensible treatment.

We also analyse our patients' lifestyles as they often hold the explanations of biological disorders.

We attempt to reduce the cardiovascular risk factors we discover to a minimum by promoting certain healthy eating habits or, for example, by recommending against harmful lifestyles. This means intervening directly in the lives of our patients and their environments.

Well, that is exactly what Guardiola did. He listened to his patient, analysed him and made an appropriate diagnosis. His patient, who displayed no signs of cardiovascular risk factors, required several therapeutic applications in order to bring to life the athlete within himself and his athletic abilities in principle.

And he was successful in doing this. He achieved a contagious balance that will hopefully have an impact on other areas of the sporting world.

Guardiola filled in working days that had been minimalistic and had little depth up to that point. He introduced group discussions, joint meals, healthy nutritional habits, videos and rules governing behaviour.

This means he used measures that were by no means new in sports but absolutely novel at FC Barcelona to reach a perfect balance, a balance between effort and recovery, a balance between demands and contentment.

And his results were optimal in every area. There was a positive group attitude, anticipation, desire and a highly favourable injury rate. All of the successes on the pitch resulted from all of this. This was the source of the titles (seven in two years) that were the coronation and an expression of the good work of Guardiola and his carefully selected staff.

Winning the titles brought about collective and historically remarkable jubilation.

I was personally most excited about its unique style: a blend of passion and rationality.

His career as an athlete and professional will be characterised by his dogged drive to learn and to find the best strategy for what is known as beautiful football, an intelligent and creative playing style that highlights both the virtues of the group as well as the abilities of individuals.

Psychologists say that compulsive disorders in adults can result from skipping a phase of personal development in childhood. Guardiola experienced all of the phases of development in full awareness. This is what gives him his professional and interpersonal skills for successful group leadership.

My profession has caused me to be very fixated on humanist values. For me, the method I want to use to achieve something comes before the result.

Well, Guardiola's performance in both areas are deserving of commendation. On top of that, he created a lesson or even a school. It is a school based on the meticulous and comprehensive preparation of athletes.

Furthermore, he uses a humanistic blend of technical skills and human behaviour.

This is his way of challenging us to play with insight.

MIGUEL ANGEL, HOW DID YOU EVEN DO THAT?

by Xarli Diego, radio commentator, former sports reporter, moderator of 'El joc del siglo' ('The Game of the Century') on TV3 and communications consultant

This book is actually deserving of many commentators, actually one for every title that Barça has won.

However, there ended up being one at the beginning of the book and four at the end (which sounds a little like the tactics of a team set up for defence). Treating five friends to dinner is not the same as treating many more. After all, we are living in times of crisis and will all end up eating at McDonald's in suit and tie. He could have actually asked me to do the foreword only, but maybe the author of this book, Miguel Angel Violán, thought a single commentary for this work could upset its balance and that it would be better to create a balance by involving other calmer individuals.

However, I am grateful to Miguel Angel as always for putting me on his list of commentators for his books even if lists and payrolls are more the thing for banks nowadays. In any case, Miguel Angel has a lot of credit. Furthermore, he has not merged with anyone and will also not be seized by the police. I have managed to observe that many books have no forward or epilogue whatsoever and that others in contrast have a sort of introduction. Then there are also books that come directly to the point. This book has everything. Miguel Angel has always liked doing everything the right way as he is a noble gentleman.

For the sake of completeness, it should also be noted (between you and me) that there are also books that are actually not worth publishing.

Well I don't actually know so well whether I should write a commentary, a long email or a letter to the Christ child. In any case, I am one of those who are happy about having an exceptional Barça with an exceptional Pep Guardiola who is certainly the cause for this upswing. We are actually still amazed that things have changed in such a fundamental way (as it was not so long ago that we were constantly in second place...do you still remember?).

Without a doubt, Barça is an entire conglomerate of feelings and sensations.

I can still remember organising a tour from my home city Terrassa to Barcelona to watch the game for the Trofeo Joan Gamper when I was 16 years old. In the end, I was the only participant. It was my first time in Camp Nou and also my first time driving to the big city on my own. When Miguel Angel asked me to write this epilogue, I again remembered the weekly recordings of teacher Joaquim Maria Puyal for the Fútbol en català (Catalan Football) programme on Barcelona FM. They were called Esta es nuestra jugada (That Is Our Play). When Puyal transferred to Catalunya Ràdio, I became the one who did the advertising for the station's Barça broadcasts. A lot of water has passed under the bridge since those days.

I can also remember participating in a very special lunch when it was decided that the Barça coach at that time, Terry Venables, should sing 'I've Got You Under My Skin' by Frank Sinatra with La Trinca during the No passa res (Nothing happened) programme on TV3.

In addition to Terry Venables, player Julio Alberto was also at the lunch (who pulled the coach to the table by his ear where he allowed me to look like a well-educated person) along with the members of La Trinca and several others.

Oddly enough, Julio Alberto wore number 4 on the pitch just like Guardiola did after him. I once assisted Julio Alberto in recording an album with his first wife, and I must admit that is was a very difficult moment for the world of music.

Julio Alberto was a very jovial person, and I am truly happy that he has since returned to normality and has begun working with Barça's youngest youth players who will go on to be future Xavis and Iniestas.

These young lads are the ones Miguel Angel Violán calls the 6:2 generation. In other words, they are capable of achieving any objective when they approach it methodically. They are the new Catalonia.

That is exactly what Miguel Angel (a passionate advocate of methodology) is talking about in this book: the method. It is a method that enables us to lead and triumph. It is the Guardiola method.

Miguel Angel Violán possesses the ability to write seamlessly. His press assignments and his activities as a columnist for Avui have only served to further refine this skill.

By the time I figure out how to open Microsoft Word on my computer's desktop, he has already written an entire page, thought of three headlines and is mulling over the fourth. He achieved all of this in a reasonable sober manner without any haste.

Miguel Angel Violán has a triple education: he is a journalist, solicitor and business economist. This allows him to enjoy a three-dimensional perspective. He can read a match in three different ways.

I can still remember very well that we spoke about a journalist's transition from mass media to the other side of the table, corporate communications, on the day we met (14 years ago). I remember his characteristic way of speaking: calm and smooth, just like it is today. Someone had told me prior to meeting him that he was an honest person, far more than others.

What shocked me was his ability to master foreign languages.

Since that first meeting, we have always kept in touch and have developed a deep friendship.

Miguel Angel understood how highly sensible it was to work for the media for a while but that one could scarcely stay there for a lifetime. That is why he transitioned to the world of corporate communications (and performed wonderful work in this field for the Riu Hotels & Resorts chain and in training people working in communications at Centre Internacional de Premsa del Collegi de Periodistes de Catalunya [International Press Centre of the Catalonia Journalists College]).

He is a man of principle, and every day he rebels a little more against the mediocrity of our society.

However, Miguel Angel is also only human and thus not all that glitters is gold. I believe that he has come to be less patient and somewhat more sardonic. As they say, I cannot write only positive things about him.

The author of this book on Pep Guardiola's leadership style is also an avid student of the topic of viral marketing. He has been posting to his Spanish-language blog, Esto es lo que hay (This is What's Happening) almost every day for the last five years. He writes about his experiences as a communicator and his trips and describes of all kinds of studies. The island of Mallorca, where he lived for 12 years, is always present in this blog.

As far as this book goes, it reveals Miguel Angel's analytical abilities. He dissects the Guardiola phenomenon and derives values and behavioural modes from it that one should follow.

For the author, Guardiola is not some sort of fascinating marginal character. He is an entire code of behaviour for a society striving for improved performance.

Despite the very one-sided nature of a football club, Miguel Angel still manages to distil ideas out of it, which are applicable to all types of organisations and companies striving to make their dreams come true.

Just as Barca has managed to do in recent seasons.

I was convinced that this book would be a success and the three editions that have been published thus far have proven me right. I was convinced because I know the author, his precision and his unique sensitivity very well.

Those who discover this work can now ask after his lectures, 'Miguel Angel, how did you even do that?'

LOVE AND PRAYERS: THE 5TH PROJECT

by Felipe Cuesta, solicitor, founder and chairman of the Micro NGO Asociación Kanyakumari for Social Projects in India

I met Miguel Angel Violán in Mallorca. At that time, I was working for a well-respected hotel chain. He was its communications director and the chain was on its way to becoming a major international corporation.

I worked there as an external lawyer. We formed a beautiful personal relationship. We later exchanged views on other things that had nothing to do with the topic of our first meeting, and over time we have come to be bound by a deep friendship.

I have always felt the desire to dedicate time and personal effort to the poorest of the poor. Possibly this comes from the fact that I was born in a small village in the province of Burgos. For many years, I was the only person there who had the good fortune of being able to attend university.

I met fellow students at the University of Oviedo with whom I altruistically dedicated myself to the task of bringing more culture to our mining regions (including Ciaño, Sotrondio and Mieres). We were united by a spirit of solidarity that drove us onward. We expected nothing in return but the satisfaction we felt in doing something for others.

After my professional career came to an end, I decided to dedicate myself to other things. As a young man, I had spent five years learning a trade, and I thought that that might be a new challenge. I was invited to teach Indian school children attending their last year of school before university. I lived there for a while and met people who lacked the most elementary things.

When I returned to Spain, I decided to help the poorest of the poor and founded the Asociación Kanyakumari, a micro NGO bearing the name of the city where I had lived.

This desire moved me and my wife Margaret to put our compassion of solidarity into practice and attempt to help the poorest of the poor: impoverished children from the Jharkhand forests, the elderly, homeless people and disabled people from Tamil Nadu and other places where we had witnessed human misery.

I was able to share these experiences with Miguel Angel Violán who had the patience to listen to me and show interest in our concerns. Moreover, he made them his concerns. He advised us on how we could better publicise the work of our NGO and presented us as a charitable association at the Business School where he worked as a lecturer. He also recommended us to his friends. He asked them to donate to the four projects that we currently maintain in India instead of giving him gifts for his 50th birthday on 18 January 2009.

We have since begun work on our fifth project: building an orphanage. Miguel Angel has also embraced this and has offered to dedicate the revenue from the sales of the Catalan edition of his book on Pep Guardiola to the project. Guardiola has come to be celebrated by all football lovers and even the fans and supporters of opposing teams. His qualities have been recognised and acknowledged.

With these objectives in mind, my wife Margaret and I would like to thank Miguel Angel for his generosity and demonstrate our affection and friendship to him.

We would like to take this opportunity to send him love and prayers as our Indian friends do when they greet us. We also do this in the name of the children who can be taken into the orphanage as their only refuge. This place will become reality with the help of all of those who purchase this book or would like to collaborate with the association.

We thank you from the bottom of our hearts. Love and prayers.

Madrid, 21 May 2010

http://www.asociacionkanyakumari.org

APPENDIX ▪ ▪ ▪

JOKES ABOUT MADRID AND BARÇA

Feats of athletic heroism vis-à-vis great rivalries usually entail all sorts of amusing commentaries, jokes and biting statements.

Barcelona's 6:2 victory on 2 May 2009 at Bernabéu Stadium produced a great number of these. The majority were of a more transient nature even if they did have a certain charm that brought smiles to all of our faces.

In this regard, I recall a remark by a Real Madrid board member in the stands at Bernabéu after the final whistle of the game,

'Goodness, you played like the Harlem Globetrotters!'

This speaks of a very authentic sort of humour that expresses recognition, accepts the defeat in a nice way and congratulates the opponent.

There were also more biting jokes to be heard among the blue-red fans who wanted to rub salt in the wound (or eye) of the Madrid fans. These jokes circulate rapidly online and serve as evidence of how euphoria can promote a derisive sort of creativity. Here are some examples:

1. ¿En qué se parece el Barça a una empresa de la construcción? Pues en que el año pasado le hizo el pasillo al Madrid, y este año le ha hecho el baño. What do Barça and a construction company have in common? Last year it remodelled the hallway in Madrid, and this year it remodelled their bathroom.

2. Do you understand what two Catalans, an Argentinian and a Frenchman do? No?? Neither does Madrid's defence!

3. Why does the whole world call Iker Casillas an 'internet junkie' after the 2:6 game? Because he's always on the net!

4. What does the 2:6 Real Madrid squad have in common with a crèche? Both are full of figures that stand there motionless.

5. Why was Madrid's next game rescheduled for a Saturday? Because football is played on Sunday!

6. Who knows when the next set will be played after the 2:6?

7. Why do the people in Madrid go to mass every Sunday? Well, they want to see someone in white holding up a cup.

8. Who would Madrid have signed if the score had already been 2:6 at halftime? Rafael Nadal to play catch-up in the second set!

9. Why is Casillas not cold in winter? Because he plays with 10 nightcaps!

10. ¿En qué se parece el Madrid a un Dj? Pues en que se pasa toda la semana entrenando para «pinchar» el sábado. What does Real Madrid have in common with a DJ? They both train all week to spin on Saturday.

11. What does Madrid have in common with a boat full of refugees? When they catch sight of them in Europe, they send them home.

12. Why is the Spanish national team called a 'circus'? Because its line-up includes the magicians from Barça, the lions from Bilbao and the clowns from Madrid.

You can draw your own conclusions regarding the humour of the masses in the exuberance of the 6:2 victory.

Victory gives wings to the imagination of the masses. Euphoria is the best breeding ground for malicious humour.

CREDITS ▪ ▪ ▪

Cover design:	Claudia Sakyi
Cover photo:	© imago-sportfotodienst
Typesetting:	Kerstin Quadflieg
Photos:	© dpa picture-alliance (p. 17, 24, 37, 43, 62, 90, 97, 109, 113, 118, 119, 122, 138, 142, 146, 149, 160, 168, 172, 177, 181, 182, 193, 202, 210, 218, 222, 236, 247) © imago-sportfotodienst (p. 6, 22, 28, 46, 69, 72, 80, 98-99, 102, 127, 133, 134, 145, 164, 186, 243, 244) © thinkstock/iStockphoto (p. 248, 260)
Copy editing:	Elizabeth Evans

SHANE STAY

WHY AMERICAN SOCCER ISN'T *THERE* YET

MEYER & MEYER SPORT

CHAPTER

1

INTRODUCTION

The United States men's national team will inevitably lose early in the World Cup, and then the questions will begin: What are we doing wrong? How can we get better?

American soccer will someday be a consistent power like Brazil, Germany, and Argentina. However, in the past and currently, the majority of American players have some sort of built-in counteracting mechanism when it comes to creativity on the field. How can the men's national team get over this? How can America, as a soccer-playing nation, get over this?

To improve soccer in America there are many things that will need to change. In order to answer this creativity problem America faces in soccer, the following is a broad guideline to a few salient points that will need to be recognized.

In order to improve as a soccer nation, we must:

1. Encourage players to dribble.[1]
2. Encourage players to be creative.
3. Encourage players to improvise with each other.
4. Have players practice shooting inside a racquetball court.
5. Construct futsal courts and beach soccer courts in the major cities around the country.

---

1   To understand this skill, know Anson Dorrance's method of success.

6. Have players play futsal and beach soccer as much as outdoor soccer.
7. Emphasize passing the ball back to the player that just passed to you.
8. Ensure all four defenders are skilled.
9. Emphasize with the defenders that everything starts in the backcourt.
10. Emphasize with the defenders that offensive success depends on the backcourt.
11. Encourage inside defenders to study film of Franz Beckenbauer.
12. Encourage outside defenders to attack, attack, attack, dribble, dribble, dribble, and shoot, shoot, shoot (studying film of Jorginho and Cafu).
13. De-emphasize crossing.
14. Emphasize posting up forwards with their back to goal and improvising.
15. Emphasize playing across the field.

Because soccer in the United States is growing more popular, the next generation of dads will pass on skills and confidence to their sons. Major League Soccer (MLS) will give kids hope and confidence in their personal future and a decent example of how to play.

***

ISBN: 978-1-78255-028-0

AVAILABLE IN BOOK STORES AND ON WWW.M-M-SPORTS.COM